PHONO-GRAPHIC
TRANSLATION

The series of volumes,
of which this is the second,
is inscribed to the memory of
Dr. Mont Follick

MONT FOLLICK SERIES
VOLUME II

PHONO-GRAPHIC
TRANSLATION

W. HAAS

MANCHESTER
UNIVERSITY PRESS

MANCHESTER UNIVERSITY PRESS
316–324 Oxford Road
Manchester M13 9NR, England

ISB NO 7190 0394 6

11652

Printed in Great Britain by
Butler & Tanner Ltd, Frome and London

CONTENTS

Introductory   *page*

I LETTERS AND SOUNDS   3

   1. ALPHABETIC WRITING AND PHONETIC
      TRANSCRIPTION   3

   2. PHONO-GRAPHIC CORRESPONDENCE   7
      2.1. *The Referential Interpretation*   9
         2.1.1. *'Indirect Meaning'*   10
         2.1.2. *'Phonic Meaning'*   14
      2.2. *Translatability*   16

   3. GRAPHEMIC AND PHONEMIC REFERENCE   23

II 'WRITING DOWN' AND 'READING
    ALOUD'   30

   1. RECOGNITION—TRANSLATION—
      REALISATION   31

   2. THE GRAPHIC OPERATIONS   33

   3. THE PHONETIC OPERATIONS   36

   4. PHONO-GRAPHIC TRANSLATION   40
      4.1. *The Task*   40
      4.2. *Ranges of Choice*   44
         4.2.1. Kinds of disjunctive correspondence   44
         4.2.2. Distribution of the burden of choice   50
      4.3. *Controlled Choice*   56
         4.3.1. Types of clues   56
         4.3.2. Tendencies   60
         4.3.3. Rules   62
         4.3.4. Logographic and logophonic conven-
             tions   75
         4.3.5. Applications   83
      4.4. *The Untranslatable*   85
      Bibliography   89
      Index   92

PHONO-GRAPHIC TRANSLATION

INTRODUCTORY

Writing and reading, like speaking and listening, are practical skills which we do not quite understand. To be able to do something is very different from knowing what one is doing. Indeed, the two kinds of achievement tend to conflict with one another: the more skilled we become in performing an operation, the further recedes our explicit knowledge of it. In being required constantly to pass from sounds to letters, and from letters to sounds, we are in the situation of a truly bilingual interpreter. As he knows very little about problems of translation—he solves them before they appear—so the very skill we have in changing from one medium to the other hides their relations from us. We did of course have some immediate experience of them when we first acquired our written language. But this was long ago, and we cannot remember. Only theory and experiment can retrieve what has been lost to our memory. And retrieval is required for some very practical purposes.

Those who have the task of *teaching* children to read and write must somehow recover a sense of those first efforts—an awareness of the problems of writing the sounds, and sounding the letters.—The same kind of explicit knowledge will be needed —though less urgently—by those who wish to 'bring up' computers to read and write. What they really know so far is only the 'input' and 'output'; while of the operations which lead from the one to the other, they do not know enough to be able to 'write the programme'.—Spelling reformers, who aim at improving the efficiency of our alphabetic conventions, cannot possibly arrive at any reliable estimate of competing proposals, unless they fully appreciate the essential functions of such conventions. In fact, that peculiar 'bilingualism' of a literate society is bound to give rise to a variety of problems. Sociologists and politicians, psychologists and speech-therapists, writers, translators, and literary critics may all have occasion, for one reason or another, to seek a clearer understanding of the basic relationship between language spoken and language written, and of our transactions between the two.

I

LETTERS AND SOUNDS

Whenever questions are asked about the relation between alphabetic writing and speech, it is usual to refer to a model— in both senses of the word 'model': *phonetic transcription*, being simpler than any orthography, is supposed not only to elucidate the relation between alphabetic writing and speech, but also to be itself the most efficient way of relating the two. A broadly phonetic ('phonemic') transcription is regarded as the ideal alphabet. Any orthography, established or proposed, is judged against this standard of excellence. This view has rarely been challenged; but it is, to say the least, a gross over-simplification.[1]

1. ALPHABETIC WRITING AND PHONETIC TRANSCRIPTION

Phonemic transcription and alphabetic writing are of course closely related; but it is easy to see why the former is unlikely to be a good model for the latter. The two serve different purposes; phonemic transcription serves linguistic analysis, alphabetic writing serves communication.

Alphabetic orthography is an *application* of phonological analysis to a task of communication; and, like other technologies, it draws upon contributions from more than one discipline. Various non-phonological factors need to be taken account of. Some of these are linguistic; they are part of the setting of the phonological system within *the language as a whole*. Others are not linguistic; they are part of the setting of the whole language within *the life of a community*. It follows[2] that if we try to do justice to the total situation, i.e. to the grammatical

---

[1] Most eminent among the few who have subjected this view to critical scrutiny is Professor J. Vachek (cp. his *Some Remarks on Writing and Phonetic Transcription*, 1949, reprinted in *Readings in Linguistics*, Vol. II, University of Chicago Press, 1966).

[2] Cp. 'On "Spelling" and "Spelling Reform" ' in *Alphabets for English*, Mont Follick Series, vol. 1, pp. 9, 19f.

and lexical as well as the social conditions, in which a phono-logical system operates, we shall often find it advantageous for an orthography to deviate from a phonetically faithful repre-sentation of speech. For speech is more than sound, and com-munication is more than speech.[1]

Phonological analysis does of course make the central con-tribution: the reduction of infinitely many utterances to a few phonemic elements is basic to the economy of alphabetic writing. This economy being its distinctive virtue, we have to acknowledge that any deviation of alphabetic writing from phonemic transcription will be some sort of loss. Yet, though such 'phono-graphic divergence' must detract from the script's economy, it need not constitute a flaw in its overall efficiency. The 'lower-level' drawback of phono-graphic divergence may be balanced, and more than balanced, by 'higher-level' advantages: either by increasing the capacity of the orthography for signal-ling lexical and grammatical values, or by extending its social and cultural use.

In every case, then, of *phono-graphic divergence* (i.e. of ortho-graphic deviation from a phonemic transcription), we shall have to ask whether or not the loss of phonological economy is made good by non-phonological advantages. This question turns out to be more complicated—but also, perhaps, more interesting—than might have been expected. There seems to be no simple scale for measuring the disadvantages of phono-graphic diver-gence. This appears at once if we look at the difficulties encoun-tered by children or foreigners in trying to read and write English.

Firstly, some of the divergences cause more serious difficulties than others. (For example, the convention that *t* for *ten* and *h* for *hen* form a digraph *th* (/ð/) for *then* seems to be learned more easily than the convention that *g* for *gold* and *h* for *hold* form a digraph *gh* (/f/) as in *laugh*.)

Secondly, the difficulties are frequently not the same in read-ing and writing. (For example, although a child may learn fairly soon to read the *-ed* of *waited* and of *jumped* as required,

[1] It is not surprising that one of the few studies to do justice to the complexity of questions of orthography is a publication of the United Bible Societies, cp. *Orthography Studies (Articles on New Writing Systems)* by William A. Smalley and others (1964).

i.e. as /-ɪd/ and /-t/ respectively, he may continue for a long time to write *jumpt.*)[1]

Thirdly, what is difficult for the foreign learner may be easy to the English-speaking child, and *vice versa.* (For example, the representation of the English plural by -(*e*)*s*—as in *cats, cows, horses*—phonologically deviant though it is, presents no serious reading difficulty to the English-speaking child, but will be mispronounced by many foreigners learning to read English. On the other hand, the writing of *gh* in *laugh, light, right,* etc., will be easier to the adult German learner, who relates it to his own *ch,* than it can be to the English child.)

It is difficulties of this kind that concern us in judging the efficiency of an orthography—difficulties which are not necessarily the same for writers and readers, or for native speakers and foreigners, and which vary from case to case. Clearly, then, our judgment can never be based on any mere count of phonographic divergences. These need to be variously *weighted,* and the question is, how to weight them.

There will be a place in this for educational tests. A statistical survey of mistakes could enable us to assess the degree of difficulty in any particular case. The greater the difficulty the more mis-spellings. Such surveys have in fact been made. The results, however, have been disappointing; the reason being, it appears, that a mere survey of a multitude of particular cases cannot be very informative. Having made it, we should still not know how to interpret it. The mistakes are numerous and varied; and an arbitrary classification of them, such as a list of mistaken additions, omissions, substitutions, etc., will reveal nothing. There is no reason to assume that the numbers of mistakes under these rubrics will be correlated in any way with underlying difficulties of the orthography.[2]

---

[1] This difficulty is evidently connected with the fact (recently discovered) that, even within the spoken language, children acquire the allomorphic variant /-ɪd/ much later than /-d/ and /-t/. The same is true of plural /-ɪz/ as compared with /-z/ and /-s/. See Jean Berko, 'The Child's Learning of English Morphology', in Saporta (ed.): *Psycholinguistics, a Book of Readings,* 1961.

[2] The uninformative poverty of present-day studies in this field appears clearly from a survey which, though compiled in 1940, is regrettably not out of date—Georg Spache, 'Critical Analysis of Various Methods of Classifying Spelling Errors', *The Journal of Educational Psychology,* vol. 31 (1940), pp. 111–34, 204–14.

An arbitrary classification, even if it is exhaustive, is no sufficient basis for an experimental test. A count of mistakes will not be informative unless it sets out to investigate some well-founded expectations; and the expectations will be well founded if they are based on reasonable assumptions about the underlying conditions of mistakes. No doubt, a very general underlying condition will be phono-graphic divergence itself. But it can only be one among others. There seem to be good reasons, after all, for *expecting* the phono-graphically deviant *th* /ð/ to cause less difficulty and fewer mistakes than the equally deviant *gh* /f/. The conditions in which writers and readers operate seem to be significantly different in these two cases. But what, exactly, are the conditions? We might assume that ⟨th⟩ for /ð/ is easier because it has no rival, while ⟨gh⟩ for /f/ competes with ⟨f, ff, ph⟩; or also that ⟨th⟩ for /ð/ is easier to remember because it is more frequent, being a phonological marker of 'deictic' words such as 'the, this, that, there, then, thus'. These are the kinds of assumption that need to be investigated by specially designed tests. And we shall have to ask, in general terms, what *sorts* of condition are to be regarded as significant, i.e. likely to cause mistakes. It is only in the light of explicit hypotheses of this kind that a survey of spellings can become informative. Having counted mis-spellings separately for every set of significant conditions—these sets being always kept open to revision—we should be able finally to arrive at the required weighting of phono-graphic divergences.

Clearly, this weighting is no simple matter. Reasonable expectations are not easy to come by. Hypotheses do not emerge miraculously from haphazard observation. Without reference to some kind of general theoretical framework, we cannot know what to look for, or how to interpret what we find. In the last resort, only an adequate theory of the relationship between writing and speech can enable us to determine what questions are worth asking about any particular divergence between the two media. The present study originated from an attempt to provide such a theoretical framework.[1]

[1] An earlier version has been circulated among colleagues, and I am especially indebted to D. J. Allerton, A. C. Cruttenden and K. James for their patient examination of the text and for many valuable suggestions, also to Professor C. E. Bazell, as always, for stimulating comments and to Mr. MacCarthy and Mr. French for suggesting some improvements.

2. PHONO-GRAPHIC CORRESPONDENCE

I have been content, so far, to describe a phonemic transcription as 'a faithful representation' of speech, and accordingly any kind of alphabetic writing which diverges from it as 'less faithful'. But what exactly are the relations between writing and speech which are described in this way?

In one sense, nothing could be more familiar to us than this relation; we are constantly making use of it, when writing down what is spoken, or when reading aloud what is written: we have easy *practical* knowledge of it. But, as in many other cases, our *theoretical* insight into just these relationships with which we constantly operate appears to be dim and patchy.

We might approach the problem by describing the basic relation in a way which, though not informative enough from an operational point of view, would at any rate, seem to be non-controversial: namely describing it in terms of *correspondence*. We shall say then that in the case of an alphabetic script, a linear order of graphic elements ('graphemes') is generally found to correspond to a temporal succession of segmental phonological elements ('phonemes').

A phoneme, we shall have to remember, is not just one individual sound; it is a class or type of such sounds. Similarly, a grapheme is not an individual letter occurring in some particular place, but a class or type of such letters.

The correspondence, then, is between types of sounds (phonemes) and types of letters (graphemes).

In a phonemic transcription, the correspondence between the two sets is *one-to-one*: i.e. to every phoneme there corresponds one and only one grapheme, and to every grapheme, one and only one phoneme. It is on account of this that a phonemic transcription can be said to be a faithful visual representation of the auditory structure of speech. This is what enables us to discuss phono-graphic divergence, i.e. any deviation from a one-to-one correspondence between graphemes and phonemes, as if it were a divergence between two *scripts*, an orthographic and a phonemic, though, in fact, we must be taken to be referring ultimately to a structural divergence between the orthographic text and *speech*.

Phono-graphic divergence in an alphabetic convention,

then, means that the correspondence between graphemes and phonemes is *not one-to-one*, but is either

(*a*) *one-to-many*—for example, the correspondence of ⟨c⟩ in *cat* and *cider*—to different phonemes, /k/ and /s/,

or

(*b*) *many-to-one*—for example, the correspondence of ⟨c⟩ (cat) and ⟨k⟩ (kitten) to one and the same phoneme /k/,

or, indeed, as in the case of English orthography, it is

(*c*) both, i.e. *many-to-many* (Figure 1).

Figure 1

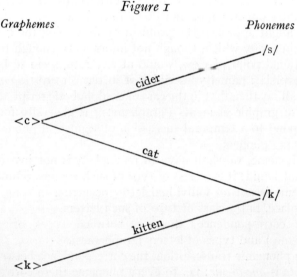

NOTE: Graphemes are written between angles, ⟨ ⟩, phonemes between slant lines, / /.

This kind of mapping must be basic to any study of the relations between alphabetic writing and speech. It provides us with an orderly account of agreements and differences between the two media. But more is required. A description of phonographic relations in terms of correspondence between dead inventories of phonemes and graphemes will not be sufficient for our purpose. In examining the transactions of 'writing down what is spoken' and 'reading aloud what is written', we are concerned with the active tracing out of those correspondences in either direction. We are asking about *operations* performed upon the 'corresponding' inventories. Is there anything more we could say about these operations?

2.1. THE REFERENTIAL INTERPRETATION

It is tempting to try to provide for the operational use of phoneme-grapheme correspondence by interpreting it in *semantic* terms. We might then say that the graphemes are *signs* of phonemes—that they *refer to* sounds, and have, in this sense, *referential meaning*. Phono-graphic correspondence would then be interpreted as *'phono-graphic reference'*.[1] The ultimate elements of written utterances would not be meaningless, then. Unlike the phonemes, to which they correspond, they would be *signs*—though not of anything outside language. They would be signs precisely of those phonemes. Let us look at some of the consequences of this approach!

First, as regards the supposed semantic value of graphemes— what Professor McIntosh calls their 'phonic meaning': deviations from one-to-one correspondence to phonemes will now have to be thought of as analogous to the familiar semantic deviations of homonymity and synonymity. Thus,

(*a*) correspondence of the same ⟨c⟩ (of *cat* and *cider*) to two different phonemes will be analogous to homonymity, and ⟨c⟩ might be said to be 'ambiguous'; and

(*b*) correspondence of both the ⟨c⟩ of *cat* and the ⟨k⟩ of *kitten* to the same phoneme will be analogous to synonymity between signs in complementary distribution (e.g. between the *-ess* of *actress* and the *-ine* of *heroine*), and ⟨c⟩ and ⟨k⟩ might be said to be 'equivalent'.

This is at first sight attractive. But as one tries to think out this referential interpretation of phoneme–grapheme correspondence, one soon discovers difficulties. If English orthography, for instance, is viewed in this way, i.e. as a semantic

---

[1] An interesting exposition of this view—with a bibliography reaching back as far as the grammar of *Port Royal*—will be found in A. McIntosh, *'Graphology' and Meaning,* 1961 ('Patterns of Language—Papers in General, Descriptive and Applied Linguistics', Longmans, 1966). I am greatly indebted to this study—not less by way of contradiction than by way of agreement.

system, we shall be puzzled to say how it can work at all. For though languages are tolerant of a great deal of referential homonymy and synonymy, there is no example of a semantic system so utterly disrupted as to make almost every one of its elements suffer from multiple splits and equivalences of meaning. Is English orthography really quite so irrational? Is it as deranged as a referential interpretation of graphemic values would make it out to be?

Though consequences such as these seem to be sufficient to refute the theory which implies them, it is still instructive to go on and examine some further implications—implications especially which will take us beyond the supposed 'phonic meaning' of graphemes, to the 'normal meaning' of such sequences of them as *cat* or *kitten*.

While the graphemes of an alphabet are supposed to be signs of some other language-material (generally phonemes), the morphemes or words, which are made up of them, clearly refer to (or engage with) things outside language. This twofold 'semantic load' covers a whole nest of problems. Basically, we have to decide here, whether the references of a written message to things outside language are *direct*, i.e. potentially independent of the spoken utterance to which it refers by its letters; or whether perhaps those extralingual references are *indirect*, i.e. always mediated by the 'phonic reference' of the graphemes? In other words: The morphemes and words of a written message, which are signs in the normal sense of 'sign' (for they carry meanings, in the normal sense of 'meaning'), and indeed the message as a whole—are they all of them only signs of signs?

2.1.1. *'Indirect Meaning'*

This theory of writing is quite clear.[1] Having distributed that twofold semantic load between writing and speech, one has disposed of any problem as to how to reconcile the two kinds of

---

[1] Many scholars have toyed with it, but some have seriously maintained it—e.g. more recently, Robert A. Hall, Jr., in *Sound and Spelling in English* (Chilton Books, 1961, 1966), p. 9, as also in his *Introductory Linguistics* (Chilton Books, 1964), pp. 263ff.

Even Aristotle is sometimes cited in support of this 'signs of signs' theory of writing; this, on the evidence of a single sentence from the beginning of *De Interpretatione*. What we find there, however, is a very

reference. Written messages are supposed to have, themselves, just one kind—the reference of letters to phonemes. It is clear then how the other kind of reference takes over when the first has landed us in the medium of speech. The only objection to this clear and unproblematic theory is that it is not true. It is simply a fact that a message can exist in *either of the two* media independently of the other. Even a language can. There is obviously speech without writing; and equally, though perhaps less obviously, it is possible, in understanding a written message, to ignore the phonetic realisation of it—or, indeed, as in the case of dead languages, to be simply ignorant of the corresponding sounds and yet understand what is written.[1] I am not saying that independence of writing is usual or even frequent, but only that it is *possible*; and this is enough to warrant us in rejecting the view that a written message acquires meaning *only via* speech.

One can understand how easy it is to be misled here. Speech is *prior* to writing in the history of nations as well as in the biography of any individual; it 'is there already' when letters are brought into relation with it, rather as cats 'are there already' before we refer to them. But the availability of cats is not only genetically prior to the use of the corresponding word, it is also *implied* by it: while the availability of sounds is never *required* for making sense of the written messages which contain the corresponding letters.

It is true that, besides being historically prior to writing, speech is, on the whole, also prior in importance. In other words, there are good reasons for the genetic priority—*bio-logical* reasons. These are so obvious that we easily forget them,

innocuous and uncontroversial statement, which says simply that 'what is spoken is a token of mental experience, and what is written down, a token of what is spoken'. The enlistment of Aristotle's support, here, requires a very special and, in the context, quite inappropriate translation of σύμβολον (token) as 'sign' in that technical sense, in which Aristotle, in fact, uses the term σημαντικόν. (Cp. p. 13, below.)

[1] The significance of this fact is not always sufficiently appreciated. The essential independence of the two 'norms', the spoken and the written, admits of important differences between them. A searching account of these differences will be found in Josef Vachek, *Zum Problem der geschriebenen Sprache* (1939), reprinted in *A Prague School Reader in Linguistics* (Indiana University Press, 1964); also A. McIntosh, 'The Analysis of Written Middle English' (*Transactions of the Philological Society*, 1965).

B

though they have been pointed out frequently: speech, but not writing, permits communication in the dark, in all directions, and, moreover, leaves hands and eyes free for other work. No wonder then that, of the two media, speech is the one more deeply rooted in our habits of communication, and that, in varying degrees, some silent form of it continues to accompany much of our writing and reading.[1]

But what does this have to do with the meaning of written texts? The fact that speech normally 'takes precedence over writing in human affairs' surely does not imply that *meaning* (in the normal sense) is 'conveyed, *not* by written shapes but . . . only by spoken morphemes'.[2] The biological and historical precedence of speech is no *logical* priority. From the fact that we had to speak before we could write it obviously does not follow that our writing can convey nothing unless it first refers to a corresponding oral utterance. But the detection and rejection of this non-sequitur—surely a matter of plain elementary logic —has often been branded as 'naïve', a 'popular misunderstanding' or 'traditional fallacy'.[2]

We may be further misled by muddles about 'representation' —as when we describe writing as a representation of speech, and think of something like mere reflection. But 'representation' in this context is a symmetrical relation like correspondence. If writing represents speech (crudely or not), it follows that speech represents writing, but not at all that writing must fall short of being itself 'a sign-system with a direct relation to the world' (Postal[2]). We might as well argue that deaf-and-dumb language can convey no meaning to those who are deaf and dumb. In Hjelmslev's words: 'The fact that a manifestation is "derived" in respect of another does not alter the fact that it *is* a manifestation of the given linguistic form [structure] . . . Diachronic considerations are irrelevant for synchronic description.'[3]

Reluctance among linguists to recognise the independent sig-

[1] Cp. Åke W. Edfeldt, *Silent Speech and Silent Reading* (1959).

[2] R. A. Hall (1961, pp. 2, 9); cp. also P. M. Postal, *Review of Dixon, Linguistic Science and Logic* (LANG, 1966, p. 91).

[3] *Prolegomena to a Theory of Language* (Madison, 1963), p. 104f. Disputing this, R. Jakobson (*Selected Writings*, vol. 1, pp. 653f.) does in fact offer only 'diachronic considerations'; though, basically, it seems to have been sensitivity to the relative limitations of written communication that suggested to him that letters 'irreversibly symbolize' sounds (with M. Halle, 'Phonology and Phonetics', op. cit., pp. 475, 654). We shall

nificance of written texts is a very recent phenomenon. It seems to be due to an 'over-reaction' against past neglect of the spoken language.[1] We are in no danger now. The time seems to have come for regaining a rational balance.

Independent significance of written messages is, in fact, a natural concomitant of the 'arbitrariness' so-called of the linguistic sign, i.e. the arbitrariness of the bond between 'signifier' and 'signified'.[2] Here, we might note, lies an important difference between language and the 'language' of music. The 'meaning' of a piece of music is obviously motivated by its component sounds. The bond between musical meaning and musical expression is not arbitrary; the auditory medium cannot be replaced without losing the 'message'. Consequently, a musical score cannot convey its meaning directly but can convey it only *via* an actual or imagined musical performance. Nor can those who are born deaf learn to understand music by reading its score, as they can learn to understand talk by reading its text.

We need not and shall not deny that something is bound to be lost by a transfer from speech to writing (though something may be gained too). But in the case of music only some general structural features are transferred to the score. No matter how exact the structural correspondence between the two media, the score remains a mere record of the musical 'signs'; it cannot be a translation of them. Music is not translatable into another medium. But speech is. While a text, too, is a record—a token of some spoken utterance, a symbol of it in Aristotle's sense of 'symbolon'—it is more: it is also a translation. Translations do, of course, vary in adequacy. Indeed, we might say of some spoken poetry that it aspires to the untranslatability of music: not just in the very limited and rather trivial way of onomatopoeia but in efforts to rescue the sounds of linguistic expression from their arbitrary insignificance, to make the meaning absorb its expression—indeed, to make anything about a linguistic expression that appears to be arbitrarily imposed: its

---

see that there is another and more satisfactory way of accounting for those limitations.

[1] But there have been unfashionable protests even twenty years ago; cp. Dwight L. Bolinger, *Visual Morphemes* (LANG 1946).

[2] F. de Saussure, *Cours de linguistique générale*—'Le lien unissant le signifiant au signifié est arbitraire' (pp. 100f.). Similarly, later, L. Hjelmslev: 'The entities of linguistic form are of "algebraic" nature and

grammar as well we its sounds, so intrinsically essential to its meaning as the auditory expression is to a piece of music. Many poems, as we meet them on the page, are then not much more than written records: they need to be read aloud. Yet, the very fact that we are able here to speak of difficulties of translation and of degrees of translatability, is surely evidence that written texts are independently meaningful.[1]

2.1.2. 'Phonic Meaning'

Of what use is it, then, to be left with that alternative account of the significance of a written text, which burdens it with *two kinds of meaning*: the 'phonic' reference of graphemes, and the extralingual reference of morphemes or words?[2] The relation between the two at once raises awkward problems about 'phonic meaning'. Graphemes turn out to be very peculiar 'signs': their semantic values do not contribute in any way towards the meanings of the expressions composed of them. Indeed, as they combine with one another in a morpheme or word (i.e. in a sign, as normally understood), their 'phonic meanings' disappear, being irrelevant precisely on account of the semantic autonomy of the written signs.

The individual letter ⟨c⟩ of 'Here's our cat' cannot be taken to refer to a certain class of sounds, in the sense in which the word *cat* refers to a certain class of animals. For if we ignore the *correspondence* of ⟨c⟩ to some sounds (and similarly with all the other letters of the sentence), the sentence remains, whereas if we ignored the *reference* of the word *cat*, the message would disappear. To say that in the case of letters 'referential meaning' is *always* contingent,[3] i.e. *always* capable of being ignored without destroying the message, amounts to admitting that letters are essentially unlike any component sign that we describe as having referential meaning. Their correspondence to sounds,

---

have no natural designation; they can therefore be designated arbitrarily in many different ways.' (loc. cit.)

[1] Cp. below, § 4.4.

[2] The most searching investigation along these lines will be found in A. McIntosh, *'Graphology' and Meaning*. J. Vachek attributes 'second order reference', via speech, only to phonetic transcriptions (*Writing and Phonetic Transcription*, op. cit., pp. 153, 155f.)—but only because these are offered as analytic descriptions of speech.

[3] A. McIntosh, *'Graphology' and Meaning*, op. cit., p. 109, n. 19.

then, ought to be described in different terms. Clearly, the letter *c* which occurs in *cat* is not a name; it is as meaningless as the sound [c] to which it corresponds.

Sounds may of course be referred to and named—as when we say: *'Cat* begins with "[kei]" '. And letters may also be referred to and named—as when we say: *'Cat* begins with "[si]" '. But no word, written or spoken, is composed of names. Spoken words consist of individual sounds; and written words, of individual letters; and between the two kinds of element there is correspondence but not reference.[1]

The relations of graphemes to one another resemble the relations of phonemes to one another; their co-occurrence within a word is not like that of morphemes within a sentence.[2]

Sounds are related to letters rather as they are to grooves on a gramophone record or to vibrations of a telephone diaphragm, all of which *correspond* to them ('represent' them, or are 'tokens' of them), but do not refer to them. The relation itself between writing and speech is different in kind from the reference of either to things outside language.[3]

The distinction which is here required between, on the one hand, reference and, on the other, phono-graphic correspondence, cannot be made satisfactorily in terms of two kinds of reference. The attempt has been made; indeed, it would be difficult to improve upon the explorations along these lines which we owe to Professor McIntosh. He cannot be accused of ignoring the differences. One of the reasons, he tells us, for treating the function of graphemes and the function of

[1] These perplexities are further discussed in section 3 below.

[2] For a 'two-meanings' theory of written texts, however, it would simply follow from the ascription of meanings to graphemes that 'the graphic categories, as compared with the phonic categories, are shifted, each time one unit along the hierarchy' (C. E. Bazell, *The Grapheme*, 1956, reprinted in *Readings in Linguistics*, Vol. II, University of Chicago Press, 1966, p. 361). Similarly, A. McIntosh (loc. cit.). We need only abandon 'phonic meaning', and those highly problematic 'shifts' disappear.

[3] This seems to be the reason why C. E. Bazell, though himself attracted by a morphemic characterisation of letters, and even by the view that graphic forms share in the expression of ordinary linguistic meaning only via phonemes, finds it necessary, nevertheless, to express doubts about 'phonemics represented as the semantics of graphemics'. 'This', he says, 'will not do. There is nothing for which morphemes "stand" in the way that letters stand for sounds.' (Op. cit., pp. 359, 361.)

morphemes as being both meanings of one kind or another, is exactly that the differences between the two 'can best be discovered under the stimulus and discipline of exploring parallels and similarities'.[1] This is in fact what we have been trying to do. But following in the steps of this intriguing inquiry, we found that the ascription of referential meaning to graphemes, with which we began, requires such qualifications as must, in the end, amount to its denial. The very relationship between letters and sounds is quite different from the relation between significant utterances, written or spoken, and the things to which they refer. This difference in relationship has, as we shall see, important practical consequences for the operations which are performed in reading and writing; these are quite unlike grasping or expressing the meaning of an utterance, though they are similar to another semantic operation.

2.2. TRANSLATABILITY

There is a sense in which one can say, quite in accord with natural usage, that a grapheme means a phoneme:—⟨c⟩ means /k/ in the sense in which French *cheval* means English *horse*. What I am going to propose is just this—that the operation which we perform upon the correspondence between writing and speech is *translation*—proceeding in one direction when we write down what is spoken, and in the other when we read aloud what is written. For, translation—unlike reference or 'mere representation'—establishes a symmetrical relation: if ⟨c⟩ is translated /k/, then /k/ is translated ⟨c⟩. This interpretation is clearly in accord with the connections we make between the two media, as well as with their mutual independence. As we can understand what is said in one language without translating it into another, so we understand what is spoken without writing it down, and also what is written without reading it aloud.

The meaning of a written text need not be mediated by speech; it is not pursued through a chain of two references:[2]

WRITING——refers to——→SPEECH——refers to——→'THINGS'

---

[1] Op cit., pp. 102f.
[2] As, for example, asserted by R. A. Hall, 1961, p. 9, and 1964, pp. 263f.

Nor does a written message carry a twofold semantic load; it does not operate in a network of three references:[1]

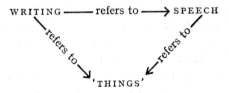

The relation between writing and speech, which (as we found) is different in kind from the reference of either of them to things outside language, is translatability:

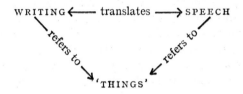

Translation has of course been mentioned frequently in this connection. But such mention seems to have served merely as some sort of incidental metaphor, vaguely elucidating an obscure operation. I wish to suggest that phono-graphic translation is to be taken seriously—indeed, literally. The *operation* is the same as in ordinary interlingual translation. But this may require some explanation.

The precise analogy between the two kinds of translation— the identity of the operation in both—will be missed as long as we rest satisfied with a vague and mysterious though very traditional view of translation. If we interpret the operation of translating as consisting in the transfer of some neutral extra-lingual meaning from one linguistic expression to another then, clearly, we shall have to say that nothing of the sort can take place when meaningless phonemes are matched with meaningless graphemes. But such a view of translation, though perfectly acceptable as some sort of explanatory myth, is quite incapable of application. The alleged operation is not performable. In order to 'transfer a meaning', we are supposed to catch it as something independent of the two languages—indeed,

[1] As suggested by McIntosh (op. cit.).

something independent of any language whatever. But since we have never met meanings outside language, we could not say what it might be like to transfer them, a host of migrant souls, from one linguistic embodiment to another. Not a single technical question about the appropriateness of a given translation, or about the relative merits of rival translations, can be tackled by reference to this 'explanatory' myth.

We do not doubt that the meaning of an expression is a mental fact. Memories and expectations are mental facts. But *what* we remember or expect as 'meaning' is not some disembodied expressionless 'pure idea'. It is our memory of an expression's past uses, and our expectation of future uses, that we are trying to match when we undertake to translate its meaning by another expression. It is such a match of remembered and expected uses (i.e. of the distinctive occurrences of two different expressions) that sanctions the translation of, say, *horse* by *cheval* in 'He bought a horse', and by *marotte* in 'Spelling-reform was his hobby-horse'. This matching of the occurrences and contrasts of different expressions *can* be described in detail; we can assess *to what extent* it succeeds or fails: while a supposed preservation of some identical 'pure' idea (of 'horsiness' or 'hobby-horsiness') in different expressions can only be asserted or denied.

Now if this is what translation essentially amounts to: a matching of expressions in their functions—then the *operation* is essentially the same, no matter whether we move from one 'medium' to another or from one 'language' to another. The difference between these two cases will be found basically not in the operation but in the kinds of element upon which it is performed. In translating, as we say, from one 'language' into another, the matching is applied on the whole to elements which in both media have meanings. In passing from one 'medium' to another, the same operation is applied, but on the whole to elements which are in themselves meaningless.

Phono-graphic and interlingual translation may often concur. For whether we shall translate sounds or translate lexical elements depends entirely upon the affinity or remoteness of the two *languages or media*; and this itself is not uniform for all pairs of sentences. The *discipline* of translation consists in matching messages (generally, sentences) *at the lowest possible level and rank*—i.e. (as we say) in making the translation as 'literal' as possible. There are cases, besides reading and writing, where this requirement is met by translating mere sounds—most conspicuously so, when we translate from one dialect into another. For example, when Cockney English /mɒɪ bɔɪ kaɪm laɪt/ is translated into Southern Standard English by /maɪ bɔɪ keɪm leɪt/, a mere matching of diphthongs: /ɒɪ/↔/aɪ/, /ɔɪ/↔/ɔɪ/, /aɪ/↔/eɪ/, yields the best translation. 'My son did not arrive in time' would be a worse translation. It is precisely because translation is possible at the lowest level that we regard Cockney and Southern Standard English as dialects of one and the same language. It is at this level, too, that translation between speech and writing operates.[1]

We shall see that such differences as there are between 'intermedial' and 'interlingual' translation—and there are many— can all be perfectly accounted for by the circumstance that translation does not operate at the same level in both. One difference especially is so important and obvious that we might mention it at once. Transfer from speech to writing, and *vice versa*, is capable of 'standardisation', some particular translation being singled out as the 'correct' one, while in translating a message from one language into another there are several possibilities—some better, some worse, and some equally good. This difference, clearly, derives from the fact that the inventory of elements, with which low-level translation operates, is a very restricted closed list, while the higher-level elements which are to be matched in interlingual translation—words, phrases and sentences—are so varied and numerous, that their choice cannot be regulated by any fixed standard.[2]

[1] Clearly, we are here concerned with translation in the accepted sense —that is, with a total matching of utterances in different media (in the widest sense of 'medium'). If, in a recent publication (*A Linguistic Theory of Translation*, O.U.P., 1965), J. C. Catford denies the possibility of 'translation between phonology and graphology', he is, in fact, not denying what has here been asserted. For he denies the possibility of what he calls 'restricted translation'. This—as he admits—is *not* translation in the accepted sense, but is a kind of *mimicry*. An example is the imitation of the sounds of one language by the speaker of another (such as Japanese /kurabu/ trying to hit off English /klʌb/ 'club'). It is obvious that ink cannot *imitate* sound. But to call mimicry 'translation', even 'restricted translation', seems to invite confusion.

[2] A fuller discussion of the general theory of translation would be beyond the scope of this paper. I have attempted this on another occasion

The 'ambiguity' and 'equivalence' of graphemes will now appear in a different light. When the correspondence between writing and speech is viewed as translatability—i.e. the ⟨c⟩ of *cider* and *cat* as transferring to either /s/ or /k/, rather than 'referring' to them, and similarly, the ⟨c⟩ and ⟨k⟩ of *cat* and *kitten* as equivalently transferring to /k/—, then we shall not ask any more how a symbolic system, in which almost every element is affected by multiple 'homonymity' and 'synonymity', could yet be workable.[1] The problem disappears when we observe that the correspondence relation

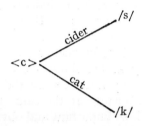

is not like the reference relation

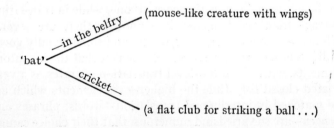

(cp. 'The Theory of Translation', *Philosophy* (July 1962), reprinted in *The Theory of Meaning*, ed. G. H. R. Parkinson, Oxford Readings in Philosophy, 1968, Oxford University Press).

[1] In *The Sound Pattern of English* (which appeared only when this study was completed) N. Chomsky and M. Halle make the rather extravagant claim that, for native speakers of English, the traditional English orthography comes very close to an 'optimal orthographic system' (49f., 184). Whatever we may think of this claim, it is clear, at any rate, that the relation by which the 'abstract representations' of such an orthography are linked to speech is not just reference; the link, after all, even with the intervening 'phonetic representations', is effected by transformational rules, which here (as, indeed, in other parts of generative grammar) are themselves rather close to translation rules. A further translation will be required to convert 'phonetic representations' into speech (cp. 25, below).

but that it is like

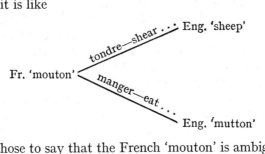

If we chose to say that the French 'mouton' is ambiguous on account of its one-many correspondence to English, we should have to be careful to distinguish this extrinsic *interlingual 'ambiguity' by translation* as altogether different from the *intralingual homonymity by reference* which affects the English 'bat'. Similarly, if we chose to say that the English 'sheep' and 'mutton' are equivalent on account of their many-one relation to French 'mouton', we should obviously have to distinguish this interlingual extrinsic *'equivalence' by translation* from cases of intralingual *synonymity by reference.*

If it is hardly conceivable that a semantic system should contain within it such extreme homonymic and synonymic confusion as a referential interpretation would impute to English orthography, there is, on the other hand, every translator's experience to confirm that almost any word of a language can be made to appear 'ambiguous', or to appear 'equivalent to others', by matching it with translations into some other language. This sort of factitious interlingual 'ambiguity' and 'synonymity', however profuse, is perfectly tolerable. It does not affect the internal working structure of the language. French 'mouton' is obviously not homonymous on account of its English translation by both 'sheep' and 'mutton', nor are these last synonymous on account of their translation by 'mouton'. The fact that there is no one-to-one correspondence between French and English words does not affect French or English, though it does of course present a problem for the translator.

Similarly with the one-many and many-one correspondences of graphemes to phonemes. The 'ambiguity' of ⟨c⟩ and the 'synonymity' of ⟨c⟩ and ⟨k⟩ are factitious, being imposed by translation. Within its own medium, grapheme ⟨c⟩ is not homonymous on account of its correspondence to /s/ and /k/, nor are these, in their medium, synonymous on account of their translation by ⟨c⟩.[1] Phono-graphic divergence, then, cannot in itself affect the working structure of either writing or speech, though it does of course present problems to the translator.

Problems of phono-graphic translation are of course a much more common concern than are those of English–French translation. Most of us are 'bilingual' with regard to the two media; speech is our 'first language', and writing has been learned chiefly by translation. Moreover, phono-graphic translation continues to occupy us throughout our lives. It is therefore all the more important, as we shall see, that the many difficulties, in education and communication, which arise from phono-graphic divergence, should be recognised for what they are—that is, as problems of translation. Recognising and treating them as such, we shall find them less confusing, and less intractable.

I am not going to suggest, though, that the transactions between writing and speech can be fully accounted for in these terms. Translation only covers the correspondence between graphemes and phonemes. Yet, in writing down what is spoken

[1] If then, in a description of grapheme-phoneme relations, we wish to speak of graphemic 'ambiguity' and 'synonymity', we shall have to remember that these terms would have to apply equally to phonemes. One-many correspondence of grapheme ⟨c⟩ to phonemes /s/ and /k/, i.e. its 'ambiguity', implies of course, as its converse, a many-one correspondence of these phonemes to the grapheme, i.e. their 'synonymity', and *vice versa*. Similarly, 'synonymity' of graphemes ⟨c⟩ and ⟨k⟩, as corresponding to one and the same phoneme /k/, implies, and is implied by, the 'ambiguity' of /k/.

We have reached a point at which it seems advisable to change our original and provisional terminology. Seeing that a grapheme could only be called 'ambiguous' in a sense in which a phoneme or, indeed, French 'mouton' would also have to be called 'ambiguous'; and that graphemes could only be called 'synonymous' in a sense in which different phonemes or, indeed, 'sheep' and 'mutton' would also have to be called 'synonymous': we should perhaps desist from straining the uses of these two terms. Instead, we might perhaps speak of the *merging* and *split* of elements by translation, and describe graphemes ⟨c⟩ and ⟨k⟩ as 'merged' in their correspondence to phoneme /k/, and grapheme ⟨c⟩ as 'split' by /s/ and /k/.

Grapheme ⟨c⟩ may be termed '*polyphonic*', on account of its being translatable by more than one phoneme; and these phonemes, /k/ and /s/, being translatable by one and the same grapheme, may be described as '*isographic*'. On the other hand, phoneme /s/, corresponding to more than one grapheme, may be termed '*polygraphic*', the corresponding graphemes ⟨s⟩ and ⟨c⟩ being described as '*isophonic*'.

or reading aloud what is written, we write not graphemes but letters, and we speak not phonemes but sounds. In order then to complete our account of 'reading' and 'writing', we have to supplement our treatment of the correspondence between graphemes and phonemes with some account of the relations, on the one hand, between graphemes and letters, and, on the other, between phonemes and sounds; and we shall again require operational interpretations of these relations. This asks for some patience. But the more explicit account should find its reward in converting a tangle of theoretical and practical problems into specific and answerable questions.

3. GRAPHEMIC AND PHONEMIC REFERENCE

As mentioned before, it is necessary to distinguish any grapheme such as ⟨k⟩ or ⟨a⟩, from the particular marks on paper, i.e. the particular *letters*, such as *k, K, a, A*, etc., which are instances or members or tokens of it.[1] The grapheme is designated by a name, such as 'kei' or 'ei' or indeed, by a sample occurrence of just the letter, in some kind of quotes, e.g. ⟨k⟩ or ⟨a⟩. This name of a class or type has of course some sort of referential meaning: it *refers to* the various letter-shapes, in, print or handwriting, which are to be regarded as instances of the grapheme. 'Kei' or ⟨k⟩ is a noun which belongs to the terminology of orthography; it occurs in statements *about* writing, e.g. in: 'We may write "kei" with a capital letter or in lower case, in Roman or in italic type', or 'The first letter of ⟨kitten⟩ is a ⟨k⟩'. It is, clearly, not this noun that occurs *in* the writing to which it refers. The initial letter or graph which occurs in ⟨kitten⟩ is not a noun; it is a physical object, which itself has no meaning.

This is easily forgotten, because our name for the grapheme is generally some instance of it used illustratively, such as 'kei' or 'ef'.[2] And yet, to confuse the orthographic noun which has

---

[1] Using here 'token' in the familiar sense in which it correlates with 'type'. It is to be noted that the reasons for considering capitals and lower-case letters to be of the same type are to be found in the distribution of the letters themselves, without any reference to their phonological translation (cp. p. 34, below).

[2] Though this is not always the case, the grapheme ⟨w⟩, for instance, is named 'double yoo', which contains no instance of ⟨w⟩.

referential meaning with the letters (graphs) to which it refers and which have no meaning, is like assuming that it is the noun, 'cat', that sits on the mat, when we refer to a cat sitting on the mat. Ancient grammarians were very clear about it; they distinguished *nomen* (ὄνομα) and *figura* (χαρακτήρ) of a letter.[1]

Analogously, the name which designates a phoneme, /k/ or '[kə]', has referential meaning and is a noun which belongs to the terminology of phonology. It is unfortunate and confusing that we often use the same inventory of names for graphemes and phonemes. Obviously, the name of a phoneme does not refer to graphic shapes; it refers to indefinitely many and various sounds. These sounds themselves have of course no meanings but are, like the letters to which they correspond, meaningless constituent elements of utterances.[2]

It is clear, then, why correspondence between graphemes and phonemes cannot be sufficient to account for the relation between writing and speech: what *constitutes* a written text is neither graphemes nor nouns designating them, but particular shapes, letters or *graphs* (or, as we might call them, making use of a familiar terminological device—'*allographs*', each of a certain graphemic type); and what *constitutes* a spoken text is neither phonemes nor nouns designating them, but particular

Figure 2

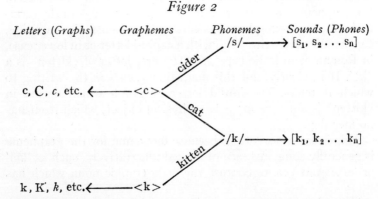

¹ Cp. Diogenes Laertius (on Zeno, VII, 56), Donatus (*Ars Grammatica*, I), Priscianus (*Inst. Gr.*, I, 6–8).
² The confusing practice of using the same name for both grapheme and corresponding phoneme may easily promote the mistaken view that graphemes 'refer to' sounds. We need only substitute phoneme 'kei' for grapheme 'kei', and 'kei' will appear to refer to voiceless velar stops.

sounds or *phones* (*'allophones'*, each being of a certain phonemic type). The correspondence relation of our diagram (p. 8) needs to be supplemented by two relations of class-membership (Figure 2).[1]

The four kinds of element will, of course, need to be distinguished equally for any convention of phonetic transcription. Graphemes must obviously be distinguished from phonemes, even if they are in one-to-one correspondence; individual letters (graphs) will differ from graphemes, no matter how stringent their standardisation may be; and graphemes will always correspond to *types* of sound, and never directly to the enormous variety of individual sounds, no matter how narrow the transcription. The same letter-symbol might of course be used for all the four units involved, the distinction being left to added markings such as brackets and subscripts; e.g. for a narrow phonetic transcription—where graphemes correspond to sub-phonemic classes such as [k]—

$$\langle k_1, k_2 \ldots k_n \rangle \longleftarrow \langle k \rangle \relbar\joinrel\relbar [k] \longrightarrow [k_1\, k_2 \ldots k_n]$$

$\langle k_1 \rangle$ being a graph referred to by the grapheme $\langle k \rangle$, i.e. by the name of a class of graphs, which itself *corresponds to* a class of sounds, the name of which, [k], refers to some particular sound $[k_1]$.[2]

This more explicit account of the relationship between

---

[1] What *kind* of class is here referred to—whether it is defined by common features of all its members or by overlapping similarities or by distribution about a central norm, etc.—this is a problem we need not discuss here. Any such class, whether grapheme or phoneme, admits of course of sub-classification, as for example in the familiar 'narrower' phonetic characterisation of /k/-sounds as aspirated or unaspirated, or unreleased, etc. allophones of the same phoneme /k/, or in the equally familiar characterisation of graphemic 'types' as capital or italic or Roman, or bold, etc. allographs of the same grapheme $\langle k \rangle$.

[2] When 'k' occurs anywhere in a meta-linguistic statement such as our diagrams, it occurs as a noun *designating graphs or sounds*. When it occurs in the 'transcription' of an utterance, e.g. in /kæt/ or [khæt], it designates nothing, but occurs as an *individual graph*, and the brackets serve as extraneous instructions for the translation of the written utterance into speech.

When we *design* a script, we are designing a language for the purpose of translating speech into another medium. This involves a naming of letters, a naming of sounds, and the establishing of correspondences between the two named types. When we proceed to *use* this new medium or language for ordinary communication, our performance will be like talk in any language: it will not be a process of designating (or referring to) successive elements of another language.

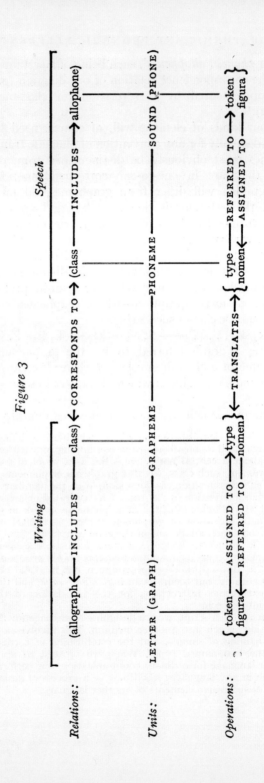

Figure 3

alphabetic writing and speech is important for an operational interpretation of it. In trying to say what we are doing when 'reading aloud' or 'writing down', we ought to make clear that, in every case, we are operating with *three relations*: with a relation of *correspondence* between graphemes and phonemes, and with two relations of class-inclusion—one between graphemes and letters, and the other between phonemes and sounds. Correspondence is generated by *translation*, inclusions by classifying operations of *assignment* or *reference* (Figure 3).

Let us note that the two classificatory operations of reference do not imply or establish any relation between writing and speech. The one assigns letter-shapes to graphemes, the other assigns sounds to phonemes. It is a very different operation that matches assigned graphs with assigned sounds. This operation, of translation, presupposes the assignments of class; we cannot match the enormous number and variety of individual graphs with the enormous number and variety of individual sounds. We are matching typical graphs with typical sounds. The two operations of reference are presupposed. But *what* we translate is clearly not these presupposed assignments or 'referential meanings'; it would be ludicrous to suggest that, in using an alphabetic script, we are engaged in matching allographic ranges (capitals, lower case, italic, and various styles of handwriting) with allophonic ranges of variation (aspirated, unaspirated, etc., and various idiosyncratic pronunciations). The translatability of letters and of sounds concerns another, third, aspect of them, besides their *figura* and *nomen*; it concerns what ancient grammarians referred to as their *potestas*—that is, their *linguistic value, as constituent elements*. What we have to match in translating from one medium into the other, is the powers which the elements (units) have, in each, for combining with one another in constituting significant utterances.[1]

The general schema is the same for non-alphabetic systems

[1] This unit of a certain value or power seems to be what Stoic grammarians referred to as στοιχεῖον, the third aspect of any 'letter', beside its χαρακτήρ (figura) and its ὄνομα (nomen) (cp. Diogenes Laertius, loc. cit.). Such an interpretation accords perfectly with the use of στοιχεῖον (element or unit) by Plato and Aristotle. It does not then seem to be a lapse of any kind (as Bywater suggests) when the term is applied equally to letters and sounds. (Cp. Bywater's edition of *Aristotle on the Art of*

c

of writing: the units will be different in value ('potestas'), but the relations between spoken and written texts, and the operation of translation, will be the same. The graphs and graphemes will here not correspond to phonemes, but to syllables or morphemes or words, or even whole sentences. We should still speak of 'graphs' and 'graphemes'. For it will be the lowest rank or level of the analysis of written utterances that will correspond here to a higher rank or level of the analysis of spoken utterances. For example, in our special and restricted notation of numbers, 3, 3 etc., are allographs of the grapheme which corresponds to the morpheme comprising the allomorphs *three, thir-* (as in 'thirteen', 'thirty'), etc. *What* we translate is again the values of the units, i.e. the powers they have of combining with one another.

The value (potestas) of graphemes, then, is determined by the general meta-linguistic principles of the writing system as a whole. The first question to be asked about any system of writing is whether the graphemes are designed to combine with one another in the way phonemes do, or in the way of syllables or words or indeed any other systematic way; the problem may be further complicated because many scripts employ graphemes from more than one of these categories.[1] The designing of a

---

Poetry, esp. 1456[6] 20, with commentary and references, p. 262.) Later, in ancient Latin Grammars, when the distinction between letters and sounds came to be more prominent, and the three aspects of a letter were distinguished as *figura, nomen,* and *potestas,* then *potestas* would seem to refer both to the correspondence of letters to sounds ('velut imago quaedam vocis literatae', Priscian, I, 4) and also to the common ground of that correspondence—including syllabic position (ibid., I, 17), morpho-phonemic alternation (I, 27ff.), and order (I, 8, 50ff.). (Cp. also J. R. Firth, *Papers in Linguistics*, p. 101.)

[1] This question is easily answered when the material at our disposal is varied and plentiful or when the problematic script can be related to kindred scripts which are understood. But it is difficult when texts are few and homogeneous in structure, and when the script bears no obvious relation to others which are themselves clear. With regard to the book-keeping tablets in Minoan Linear B, for instance, most scholars are inclined to accept that the script is basically syllabic while incorporating a modest proportion of pictograms and ideograms. But this assumption is not beyond doubt; and it may be that the ideographic or logographic element in this script is more preponderant than is commonly thought (cp. Ernst Grumach, 'Der Ägäische Schriftkreis', *Studium Generale*, 12 (1965), pp. 742–56; also 'The Decipherment of the Minoan Script B and the problem of the Linear Script A', *Man* (1957), p. 229, by W. C. Brice, to whom I am indebted for much enlightenment on this subject).

script clearly involves some kind of analysis of the spoken language, and the use of the script for reading aloud or for recording speech imposes on its users the analytic operations which are implicit in its design. The use and the learning of a purely ideographic script (such as the international road-signs) would require no more than the identification and classification of certain utterances. The use of a morphographic script (like the Chinese) imposes basically a lexical and morphological analysis of the language; in reading a text aloud or in making a graphic record of speech, we proceed here, on the whole, from sequences of graphemes to sequences of morphemes and words, and *vice versa*. On the other hand, to read or write in an alphabetic script involves primarily a phonemic analysis of the spoken utterances: we translate sequences of graphemes into sequences of phonemes, and *vice versa*; the primary elements (στοιχεῖα) in either medium are minimal distinctive segments.

Phonemic analysis is demanded of the users of an alphabetic script, even if the relation between graphemes and phonemes deviates from one-to-one correspondence as much as it does in English orthography. For even here, it is generally true of the sequences of graphemes (graphs) that they are to be translated by sequences of phonemes (sounds). It is only the case here that, generally, a grapheme or phoneme does not *by itself* uniquely determine its translation, and that the choice is often determined by grammatical and lexical characteristics of the given utterance. This does not detract from the phonemic character of the orthography; it only goes to show that, to enable one to read or write English, phonemics is not enough.[1]

We may now proceed to examine how the proposed schema may serve to elucidate the actual work of reading and writing. Having stated, in general terms, what operations are imposed on the users of an alphabet, we may try to sort out the difficulties they are liable to encounter, and the skills they are required to apply.

[1] Conversely, we find that lexical and morphological analysis is not enough for using a basically morphographic script like that of traditional Chinese orthography. It is true that, on the whole, the sequence of graphemes is here translated by a sequence of morphemes. But supplementary phonological clues are often required by the reader and are provided by the writer.

II

'WRITING DOWN' AND 'READING ALOUD'

A writing system, once established, may be used independently of speech: there is no need even for acoustic images or 'silent speech' to accompany the sequence of shapes, writing being equivalent to speaking, and reading to listening ('understanding'). Much of the skill of employing a system of writing consists in the ability to use it to a large extent without any detour, or even 'silent' re-inforcement by translation into speech—to use it, we might say, as if it were the 'first language'. I shall have little to say of this developed 'monolingual' skill, for I am concerned with the relation between the two media.

It is nearly always the case, though not necessary, that we learn our visual dialect as a 'second language', having already acquired the skill of speaking and listening. And we learn it primarily by translation—that is, through writing down what is spoken and through reading aloud what is written. In this field, the 'direct method' of second-language teaching does not seem to have been applied to any appreciable extent; it would require teachers and pupils to remain silent—as if they were learning 'deaf-and-dumb language'. Indeed, even those who adhere to a 'direct method' in teaching a foreign language would generally demand that some skill in understanding and speaking it should precede the reading and writing of it—the latter skill to be acquired *indirectly*, i.e. *via* translation.[1]

However, quite apart from the question *how* we learn to read and write—whether before being able to understand and speak or after—in almost every case, *what* we learn as written language has a spoken one to correspond to, the relations

---

[1] There are, however, occasional demands for acquiring nothing more than a command of a written foreign language—for example among the many students of scientific German or English or Russian. These requirements—the extent to which pronunciation can be avoided—do not yet seem to have been properly assessed, though to meet them may be far cheaper and more efficient than the construction and provision of machines for the translation of scientific texts.

between the two being traced out by 'writing down' what is spoken, and by 'reading aloud' what is written. Any study of literacy must be based on an understanding of these two processes.

1. RECOGNITION—TRANSLATION—REALISATION

We have seen that translation between writing and speech consists in establishing three relations: two kinds of class-membership, and a correspondence between the classified units. In reading aloud, we proceed from letters to sounds (from left to right, in our diagram); in writing down, from sounds to letters (right to left). It is important to note that *the operations differ according to the direction taken*: necessarily so in establishing an element as member of a class, since 'inclusion' is not a symmetrical relation, and contingently in establishing a correspondence of elements namely, whenever the correspondence is not one-to-one. The difference becomes obvious when the operations we have so far described in such terms as 'assignment to class', 'reference', and 'translation' are given some further psychological interpretation.

In reading aloud, one would begin with some given letter, *recognising* the grapheme in it, and proceed to *choose* the

Figure 4

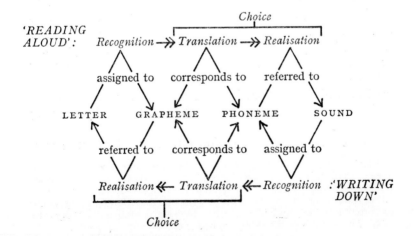

corresponding phoneme and effective sound; in writing down
on the other hand, we are given a sound, and it is the phoneme
that we have to recognise in it, while the corresponding grapheme and letter have to be chosen. The choice, in either case,
is of course not among equally appropriate alternatives. Generally, we are required to choose what is 'correct'. It is nevertheless convenient and conducive to an explicit statement of the
operations involved to view them as choice—in the sense, say, in
which we speak of choosing the right moment or of finding the
right road or ticking the appropriate answer, and the like. In
either case, it is first recognition, then choice; and the choice
is twofold—(a) the translator's choice in establishing correspondences between two media, and (b) within any one medium,
either the speaker's choice realising (giving effect to) a general
phonological concept, or else the writer's choice realising
(giving effect to) a general orthographic concept (Figure 4).[1]

Is all this making too heavy weather of reading and writing?
It may seem so. Yet, the most cursory glance at the work of a
primary school will show that the heavy weather is not of our
making. There is an abundance, here, of difficulties and of
unsolved problems. A more explicit account of *what* it is that
has to be learned is bound to be helpful for deciding how to
teach it. Clearly, both recognition and choice are involved, and
they are very different operations; and to choose a translation
equivalent is very different from choosing a token which will
give effect to the concept of some type. Each of these operations
has its problems. If we fail to sort out the various things we are
doing in reading or writing, we could not succeed even in
locating those problems. We shall find, I think, that a good deal
of what we know, as linguists or as psychologists, about recognition, reference and classification, or about problems of bilingualism and translation, has some helpful application to the
task of acquiring that most ancient and basic skill, the ability
to read and write.

We shall deal first with the operations which are performed

---

[1] J. Vachek—who clearly distinguishes the four kinds of unit or
entity involved as (a) written utterances, (b) written norm ('langue'),
(c) spoken norm ('langue'), (d) spoken utterances—describes the 'transition from one norm to the other', in the one direction (reading aloud),
as 'pronunciation', and in the other (writing down), as 'orthography'
(*Zum Problem der geschriebenen Sprache*, op. cit., pp. 442, 446).

within each of the two media, i.e. with the graphic operations (section 2, below) and the phonetic operations (section 3). Most of the difficulties which may arise here are very largely independent of whether the alphabetic system which is being used is 'phonetically regular' or not.

2. THE GRAPHIC OPERATIONS

These operations, being performed entirely within an artificial medium, are the most amenable to rational control. They can be prevented from becoming too complex, both by the original design of the script and by enforcing uniformity in its use, be it through calligraphy or through mechanical production.

As to our Roman letters, one could hardly expect them to be of the most efficient design. They carry fossilised remains of a long historical evolution, reaching back to pre-alphabetic times. But some features which are notoriously a source of difficulties—such as the right–left distinctions of ⟨d/b, p/q, s/z⟩—seem to be dictated by economy in the use of strokes and curves, and therefore not easy to avoid.[1]

Problems of design are of course far more complex in a logographic script, where graphic distinctions need to be provided for hundreds and even thousands of different elements. It is not surprising that Chinese politicians and teachers, concerned about the literacy of the people, have been trying continually to simplify the existing logographic script. (At the same time, a Chinese alphabet is being introduced, though with inevitable gradualness, only for the purpose of 'annotating' logographic texts.) Some ten years ago, in an address outlining the 'current tasks for reforming the written language', Mr. Chou En Lai cited some evidence of the need. 'A worker in Tientsin,' he reported, 'said he spent half a year in learning three characters . . . but still could not remember them. When these were simplified, he could . . .'[2] The three characters which were so

---

[1] It is remarkable that i.t.a. has augmented these difficult distinctions by adding ⟨ƨ⟩ to ⟨z⟩ and ⟨s⟩ and ⟨ʃh⟩ to ⟨ʈh⟩. Cp. MacCarthy's discussion of problems of letter-design (pp. 89–93 of Vol. I).

[2] *Reform of the Chinese Written Language*, p. 8 (Foreign Languages Press, Peking, 1958).

difficult to remember, and which even in their simplified shape remained very complex, represented just three words which that worker had to use every day. Chinese school-children have to work through a primer which introduces the first *One-Thousand Characters*.

Though our children are better off than the Chinese, we should not underrate the difficulties of graphemic recognition and realisation, even for learners of our simple alphabetic script. We find, after all, that assignment of individual letters to alphabetic graphemes is complicated enough to be still beyond the powers of any computer. We are still waiting for a really adaptable automatic reading device—that is, one that would be capable of dealing with at least the principal varieties of printed type (such as *A*, **a**, *a*, etc.), not to speak of tackling the profusion of handwritten allographs.

When we consider the full range of variants, in all of which an average reader of print and of various hands is able to recognise the same grapheme, we can see clearly that recognition is here far more difficult than realisation. Indeed, any computer can write. It cannot *write down* what is spoken, i.e. we have not succeeded yet in making a computer recognise phonemes and translate them; but a grapheme having been selected, there is no difficulty about its choosing and producing some graph to represent it.

It is true that we operate with a larger number of allographic *sub-types* than is necessary. But the principles of classification, which govern their choice, and by which we assign any of them to the appropriate grapheme, are fairly simple. For English, capitals are obligatory in a few grammatically determined types of environment (beginning of a sentence, or of a proper name, etc.) while in all other environments there is 'free variation'. This does not mean that in these other environments choice is entirely free; but—as generally in the case of so-called free variants—it is determined only by stylistic considerations, e.g. by the convention that capitals are used only for special and non-grammatical reasons (e.g. 'Block capitals, please!'). All this is fairly easy to master. The fact that German spelling-reformers have found here one of their principal issues is surely a sign that they have little to worry about. But they appear to be right in maintaining that the German conventions which impose a very extensive use of capitals are, for the most part, useless and irksome.[1] A proliferation of allographic sub-types under every grapheme seems generally wasteful, even though the skill of using them represents the easiest part of literacy.

The fact, however, that we find it comparatively easy to handle stereotyped allographs of the same grapheme has sometimes been cited to support the view that we should find it equally easy to learn the use of some additional *graphemes*— such, for instance, as might be introduced by an English spelling reform. Having found it fairly easy to use a large number of superfluous letters, we are supposed to find it equally easy to acquire a few more which are not superfluous.[2] There is, of course, a serious confusion, here. The familiar allographs such as capitals, italics, etc., are not very difficult to handle, precisely because most of them are superfluous—being 'free variants'. But addition of a new grapheme is not on a par with adding another free variant. While there is nothing new to learn about a new free variant except its shape, there is in addition something new to learn about the *use* of a new grapheme (such as ⟨ə⟩ or ⟨œ⟩ or ⟨ɛɛ⟩): new translation-rules to comply with, and some specified phonological distinctions to observe. It is true that people tend to react to any new letter as if it were just the recognition and production of the shape that would give them trouble. And one can understand why adults already trained in an orthographic tradition should tend to react in this way. The novelty of one more shape, which does not especially trouble little Johnny, is for his father a serious disturbance of automatic skills. He will be inclined to reject a graphemic innovation, without even looking beyond his first irritation. If he did, he would be even more disturbed; the new grapheme calls upon further skills, beyond those of just recognising and producing a letter. Indeed, a new graphemic use of an old letter might cause even more trouble. This was Bernard Shaw's point: the new uses would only disappoint the expectations which are aroused by the familiar shape. Better, he

[1] Cp. L. Weissgerber, *Die Verantwortung für die Schrift* (Sechzig Jahre Bemühungen um eine Rechtschreibreform), Dudenverlag, 1964. For a different opinion, see H. A. Gleason, Jr., *Linguistics and English Grammar*, p. 185f.

[2] Cp. Sir James Pitman in *Alphabets for English*, p. 16.

thought, face the initial irritation of having to learn new letters, than the outrage of finding familiar letters 'misused'.[1]

3. THE PHONETIC OPERATIONS

The phonological operations, which answer the recognition and realisation of graphemes, are only roughly analogous. The difference between the media is not unimportant. Transitory sounds, though inevitably 'slurred' in their continuous sequence, need to be caught or produced at speed; while a sequence of letters can be as slow and discrete as we care to make it.

Spoken utterances, no matter how often repeated, can never equal in clarity the letters kept still on the page. No one realises this more vividly than linguists on 'field-work' or speech-therapists, when they are trying to locate the exact pronunciation of their informants or patients. On the other hand, there are some compensatory advantages in speech. Those configurative ('suprasegmental') features—accentual patterns, rhythms and melodies—which organise the spoken utterance, cannot be satisfactorily paralleled by the sequence of discrete letter-segments. Characteristically, suprasegmental prosodic features are generally either omitted or made to correspond to separate segments such as '!' or '?'. Whatever *Gestalt*-features might be displayed by handwriting must be largely inhibited by the demand for legibility and are, in any case, too idiosyncratic to be informative. Hence the various conventional graphic devices of poetic writing, such as verse-lines, stanzas, dots, empty spaces, etc., and the discipline of an imposed meter— all serving to exact the desired reading. Poetry does as a rule demand translation into speech. It is, as it were, domiciled in our 'first language'.

This intrinsic 'material' difference between the two media makes the two 'dialects', the visual and the auditory, differ in some of their essential *linguistic aptitudes*, each being better

---

[1] This argument is not to be taken lightly. It is further reinforced if we consider the chances which new letters would offer for introducing a graphically more efficient script. The only strong counter-argument is a social and cultural one, either against any kind of spelling reform, or at any rate only for a very limited reform which preserves continuity with the tradition. (See Vol. I, my introduction and MacCarthy, 92f.)

suited than the other for some purposes.[1] This disparity must, as we shall see, present problems, when we translate from one to the other. For the moment, however, we are merely considering how the difference between the two media must affect those roughly analogous operations which are performed within each. Clearly, the analytic recognition and realisation of phonemes in fleeting sounds must be more difficult, and far more difficult to learn, than a comparable mastery of graphemes.

It is sometimes assumed that school-children learning to read and write their own language have already mastered the phonemic part of literacy. They might be said—in terms of a question-begging and misleading jargon—to have already 'internalised' the phonological system of their language, and so to need to learn only the letters. Such a claim is certainly mistaken, no matter what brand of phonology it might be made for. The use of letters in reading and writing, demands an *analytic* phonological skill which is very different from that practical ('internalised') kind, which the child has brought with him to school. There will indeed be occasions for using his practical competency: knowledge of what is possible, and what is not (e.g. that *pneumonia* cannot begin with /pn-/) will limit the choice of sounds to be read; and while there must be instruction how to draw the letters, no training will be needed in making the sounds. Yet, the analysis of speech into successive segments cannot be regarded as being given intuitively to the speaker of a language. If it were, the origin of the alphabet would have been child's play rather than an epoch-making invention.

'Reading' and 'writing' rely on *two* taxonomies, the graphemic and the phonemic; and both have to be learned. Especially in the early stages, before force of habit takes over, reading and writing are bound to be fairly self-conscious analytic operations.

Naturally we do not clearly remember *what* we have had to learn as children. This is why teachers must find it difficult to know what, exactly, they are to teach. A reminder from *adult learners* may then be welcome. The following is taken from a recent paper by the eminent Chinese linguist Y. R. Chao:

'To one who is used to an alphabetic system of writing, it seems to be the simplest thing to talk about the sound "o", the sound "e", the sound "l" [eł], the sound "b" [biː], or

[1] See J. Vachek, *Zum Problem der geschriebenen Sprache*, op. cit.

even the sound "w" [dʌbljuː]. But to one used to a logo-graphic system of writing like the Chinese, or a syllabic system of writing like the Japanese, the nature of sound segments in the forms of consonants and vowels is not at all obvious and even seems highly abstract.'[1]

It would surely be absurd to suggest that the Chinese have unlearned a 'natural' skill. To express it in the terms of the ancient grammarians: the child is in possession of *vox*, but not of *vox literata*.

It will be acknowledged at the same time, that a *child* learning to read and write *his own* language is not in the same situation as the *educated adult* who learns to *pronounce*, as well as read and write, a *foreign* language.[2] Even so, it would be wrong to assume that the child learning to write his own language has the easier task. Dr. Follick seems to think that this is so. He recalls:

'After an hour's study—yes, only just an hour—I was able to read Spanish fluently, even without having any idea what I was reading.'

and goes on to assume:

'If that was so easy for a foreigner, even before learning to speak the language, just imagine how easy it must be for a Spanish child, of six years of age, who already speaks his native language fluently, to learn to read and write.'[3]

Dr. Follick forgets that the Spanish child has yet to master those two analytic skills of graphemic and phonemic reference which are similar for all alphabetic scripts, and which he had already acquired before he came to read Spanish. Spelling-reformers are perhaps prone to such forgetfulness. They are concentrating on efforts to make phonographic translation more regular, and so tend to think hopefully that there is no more to reading and writing than this one operation: 'improve the

---

[1] *Graphic and phonetic aspects of linguistic and mathematical symbols* in 'Structure of Language and its Mathematical Aspects', *Proceedings and Symposia in Applied Mathematics*, vol. XII (American Mathematical Society, Providence, 1961).

[2] See also vol. I, Sir J. Pitman, pp. 22, 25f., and A. Wijk, pp. 55f.

[3] *The Case for Spelling Reform* (1965), p. 126.

alphabet, and the rest will be almost automatic'.[1] A more regular alphabetic convention will indeed make it easier to teach the two taxonomic skills; but neither of them can ever be 'obvious'.[2]

The difficulties which the learner of a *foreign* language finds in trying to recognise and realise the phonemes, are as a rule not due to any lack of analytic techniques but to interference by his native tongue. The greater the phonological difference between the two languages, the more serious this interference. These are again obstacles which will be tackled more easily with the help of a 'regular alphabet', but cannot be removed by it. A Japanese learner of English, who has acquired the skills of alphabetic writing will easily distinguish the graphemes ⟨r⟩ and ⟨l⟩; he will nevertheless have considerable difficulty in distinguishing the corresponding phonemes—simply because he has no occasion to keep them apart in speaking his own language. Similarly, a German or Russian, though familiar with the graphemic differences between ⟨p⟩ and ⟨b⟩, ⟨t⟩ and ⟨d⟩, ⟨k⟩ and ⟨g⟩, etc., and even with corresponding phonemic differences in some positions, will still tend to read *mob* as *mop*, *cod* as *cot*, *wig* as *wick* and *rise* as *rice*. Clearly, then, even if the plural *lies* were written ⟨liez⟩ or ⟨laiz⟩, he would still tend to pronounce it as *lice*. A more 'consistent' alphabetic convention would warn the foreign learner of the required phonemic distinctions; but no spelling reform can relieve him of the difficulties he has in recognising these distinctions, and in making them.

School-children speaking a dialect may sometimes encounter similar troubles. It is easy enough for a Cockney-speaking child to distinguish between the occurrence and non-occurrence of grapheme ⟨h⟩; in *heart* and *art*, *hedge* and *edge*, *heat* and *eat*, etc; but he will find it much more difficult to hear this difference or to make it in his speech.

An African child who may be required to learn to read and write English, without yet having acquired literacy in his own language, will have neither the advantages of the English-

---

[1] Dr. M. Follick called his consistent alphabet 'automatic', and Mr. M. Harrison entitled a recent book on the i.t.a. experiment *Instant Reading* (Pitman & Sons, London, 1964).
[2] Cp. D. H. Stott, *Roads to Literacy*, pp. 136f.

speaking child, who knows the language, nor those of the educated foreigner, who has the taxonomic skills, and will be confronted with all their different difficulties combined. This may not be sound educational policy. Similarly, it would not seem to be desirable that English children should learn to read and write a foreign language, before they have learned to read and write their own.

We have seen that of the difficulties which arise in our exchanges between writing and speech, some affect only the 'source', and others only the 'target'; we turn now to problems of passing from the one to the other.

4. PHONO-GRAPHIC TRANSLATION

It is important to distinguish the work of translation proper from the two operations of recognition and realisation at either end of it.

4.1. THE TASK

Translation is an operation not easy to make explicit. Essentially, it seems to consist of *searching the resources of the target-language for the most articulate match*. The most articulate match will be the one which, while corresponding with the source-message as a whole, presents also the largest number of separate correspondences between the parts of 'source' and 'target'.[1] In other words, the translator will try to match the source-message, as a whole, *through* separate correspondences with the smallest possible units of it—correspondences, if possible, with every word as well as every phrase or sentence, and even with phonological elements as well as with words. This search for the most articulate match constitutes, as we have seen, the discipline of translation.

As a rule, overall adequacy sets severe limits to articulate-

[1] Thus, in most contexts, German *Heimkehr* will be better translated by *coming home* or *home-coming* than by *return*, while *Rückkehr* is not necessarily translated better by *coming back* than by *return*. And *bachelor*, as translation of German *Junggeselle*, is certainly always better than 'young fellow'. The latter, in fact, would be a complete mistranslation; it could not produce a match for any German sentence (as a whole) which contains *Junggeselle*. It follows, of course, that we should find it simply impossible to match the weak flavour of the pun in '*alter Junggeselle*'.

ness: a matching throughout the spectrum of linguistic units, right down to the phonological elements, is generally not attain- able, unless the source-language and the target-language differ merely in their medium, as in phonographic translation of the alphabetic sort, or are fellow-dialects, or are at least closely re- lated. Thus, English and German do offer some partial phono- logical correspondences, especially in the consonantal onset of words: e.g.

/st/—/ʃt/: *stands still—steht still; stone—stein; star—stern;* etc.
/gl/—/gl/: *glow—glühen; glide—gleiten; glass—glas;* etc.
/fl/—/fl/: *fly—fliegen; flow—fliessen; flag—flagge;* etc.
/w/—/v/: *water—wasser; wake—wachen; wash—waschen;* etc.

Exploitation of these possibilities is far from being trivial. It is essential when one attempts to translate poetry. What is wanted then, is of course not mimicry, but correspondence. What counts is not so much similarity of the sounds in the two languages, as a matching of their 'potestas', e.g. of the alliter- ation of *stick* and *stone,* or *still* and *stand,* or *star* and *stare.* A translator will try to parallel significant phonological features of the source, even when the two languages fail to provide regular correspondences. He would then seek some *ad hoc* match. Translation of such a common cliché as, say, 'brain drain', will not be satisfactory, unless it succeeds in matching its brevity and rhyme.[1] Frequently we may have to give up. Higher-level adequacy, which is of course always in ultimate control of our operations, can never be sacrificed for the sake of a higher degree of articulateness. French *C'est vous qui avez raison* is rendered more articulately by *It is you who is right,* but, on most occasions, more adequately by analysing it into just two units—namely, *c'est vous qui* to be matched by a stressed *You,* and *avez raison* matched by *are right.*[2]

---

[1] Translation from English into German is, for historical reasons, less fortunate with rhymes than it is with alliterations. In this case, we would experiment with, say: Gehirn/Geist/Intelligenz/Talent/ Gelehrter/ etc., on the one hand, and Entzug/Abzug/Entführung/ Beraubung/ Verlust/Schwund, etc., on the other. And we might choose *Talentschwund,* to give us, besides brevity, at least a partial rhyme (in /nt/), and also a parallel to the somewhat disreputable associations of *drain,* by setting off morbid echoes of *Gehirnschwund.*

[2] We do not, of course, match *avez* with *are* or *raison* with *right.* There is no correspondence between their separate linguistic potentials.

In problematic cases, where target-units of similar 'potestas' do not easily suggest themselves, the best among alternative translations is only discovered after several attempts. Different sequences of corresponding units will be proposed, one after another, each of them matching a different analysis of the given message; until at last we think we have found the match which combines overall adequacy with the highest degree of articulateness.

This process of trial and choice may be slow and laborious; or it may be fast, effortless and curtailed by habit. But it may surely be presumed to be imposed on us by *every* kind of translation. The skilled translator, like a man skilled at 'sums', will rise to explicit awareness of his operations only in case of difficulty. But the operations will have to be performed, even for a routine-task such as that of phono-graphic translation; it took its toll of conscious pain at the time when the skill was first acquired. When digraphs and silent letters are found to complicate the orthography of English, the objection is basically that they make it impossible for translation into speech to proceed on the assumption that the most articulate match is always the most adequate. This *is* a complication. It cannot be easy, for instance, to learn that in *nation* or *partial* or *vexatious*, ⟨ti⟩ must be selected as a unit to match /ʃ/, while in *native* or *partisan*, ⟨t⟩ and ⟨i⟩ have to be matched separately by /t/ and /i/ respectively, and in *superstitious*, translation of ⟨t⟩ + ⟨i⟩ is followed by translation of ⟨ti⟩.[1]

The hardest part of the translator's task is not analysis of the source but choice from those alternative proposals for translation of which each matches a different analysis. To review the resources of one's target-language, in search for the optimal match, must be more difficult than it is to scan the limited stretch of a given message, in order to identify possible units to be matched. Clearly, the more familiar we are with the target-language, the more manageable the task. This is why it is always much easier to translate into one's own language than it is to translate into a foreign one; and why school-children learning to be literate in their native tongue find reading easier at first than writing.

One may be tempted to conclude that, once bilingualism is

[1] See pp. 77ff., below.

complete—which is fairly common with regard to writing and speech—we should translate with equal facility in either direction. This, however, is generally not the case. The correspondences with which we operate within any given alphabetic convention are found to favour either one direction or the other, or to favour sometimes one and sometimes the other. This asymmetry of effort is easily explained, as we shall see. It derives from an asymmetry in the correspondences between the two languages.

It is clear at once that a phonographic translation, which operates with a 'phonemic alphabet', is not afflicted by any of these problems. Apart from the skills of the 'input' and 'output' operations, there is no more to learn here than a few dozen correspondences. The translation itself is child's play. Moreover, being performed at a very low level, translation will be almost as articulate as it can be. The material difference between the two media will of course still exclude the possibility of a *perfect* match; and, what is more serious, the difference of function between speech and writing must prevent the most articulate match from being the most efficient.[1] Many deviations of an alphabetic script from a phonemic transcription are worth paying the price of a more complicated translation. (It seems worthwhile, for instance, to transcribe the lip-rounded /h/ of *who* by ⟨wh⟩ to parallel *what, which, where, when, why*.) This does not mean that every intricacy of our traditional alphabetic conventions is balanced by an advantage. History, which has formed these conventions, is not altogether a rational process. The problems it has bequeathed to us are not all of them valuable traditions, and they need to be sorted out.

When reading or writing operates within a highly *irregular alphabetic convention* such as English orthography, it comes rather close to the well-known complications and uncertainties of ordinary inter-lingual translation. The two appear to have in common not only the general task of having to choose the required translation from a range of *prima facie* alternatives; they even share more specific problems, and have similar ways of solving them. We shall find that both (*a*) the principal kinds of disjunctive correspondence (4.2), and (*b*) the principal

---

[1] See 'On Spelling and Spelling Reform', in Vol. I, *Alphabets for English*, pp. 1ff., also 4.4., below.

D

considerations which determine our choice (4.3)—are thoroughly familiar to us from interlingual translation.

4.2. RANGES OF CHOICE

4.2.1. *Kinds of Disjunctive Correspondence.*

These may differ from one-to-one correspondence in more than one respect. For there are two conditions to be satisfied, if phonemes and graphemes are to be paired off in one-to-one correspondence: (i) every phoneme and every grapheme contracts one and just one correspondence, and (ii) any correspondence obtains between a single phoneme and a single grapheme. From a purely logical point of view, these two conditions are quite independent. We may fulfil the second condition ('single correspondents') without fulfilling the first by 'pairing off' elements of two sets P and G as follows:

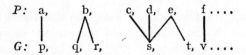

where b corresponds to either q or r, and s to c or d or e, and e to s or t. And we may fulfil the first condition ('just one correspondence') without fulfilling the second; e.g.

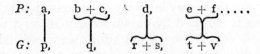

where it is true, for instance, of b or c that each contracts one correspondence only, but they do so jointly. In the special conditions of phoneme-grapheme relations, however, any failure to satisfy condition (ii)—for instance, by the use of 'digraphs'— generally goes together with a failure to satisfy condition (i): the reason being that the elements contained in a sequence such as a digraph are generally also paired off separately.[1] Deviations from one-to-one correspondence are then of two kinds. They

---

[1] Even if one element of a sequence is never translated by a separate phoneme—as in the case of ⟨ь⟩ in Russian orthography—the implication of disjunctive matching remains true for the rest. (Cp. p. 46, n. 1, below.)

may consist in failing to satisfy (i) *only*: examples are the cases cited above of /k/ being paired disjunctively with either ⟨c⟩ or ⟨k⟩, and of ⟨c⟩ being paired with either /k/ or /s/. And there may be failure, in addition, to satisfy condition (ii)—for instance, in the pairing of /k/ with ⟨ch⟩ in *school*, or of /ʃ/ with ⟨sh⟩ in *ship*, or in the other direction the pairing of ⟨x⟩ with /ks/ in *box*. We note that the matching of ⟨ch⟩ (*school*) with /k/ adds NIL to the other correspondences of ⟨h⟩, and the matching of ⟨sh⟩ (*ship*) with /ʃ/ adds some special translation-values to the other correspondences of ⟨s⟩ and ⟨h⟩. English orthography abounds in deviations of all these kinds.[1] It seems worthwhile to examine more closely what the difference amounts to in terms of translation.

When phoneme-grapheme correspondences are disjunctive merely on account of some phoneme or grapheme occurring in more than one 'pair', then the translator, having made his choice from a certain number of alternatives, will match the elements of source and target one by one: e.g. ⟨cat⟩—/kæt/ or ⟨city⟩—/sɪtɪ/. Let us call this '*element–element translation*'. On the other hand, when an alphabetic convention further deviates from the second condition of one-to-one correspondence, then what is a single element in one medium will be translated by a sequence of elements in the other. We may call this '*element–sequence translation*'. This is, of course, extremely common in the usual practice of translating from one language into another. We shall see that even here, element–sequence translation generally goes together with a special disjunctive correspondence of the parts in the sequence.

At this point, it is necessary to keep clear what is meant by 'sequence'. The common term 'digraph' covers only some of the sequences established by translation, and is in any case not clearly defined. In English orthography, is ⟨qu⟩ a digraph? Again if the continuous ⟨oe⟩ of ⟨toe⟩ is a digraph, is the discontinuous ⟨o . . e⟩ of ⟨tone⟩ also one? And shall we extend the term to cover larger sequences such as ⟨ssi⟩ of ⟨mission⟩, or ⟨ough⟩ of ⟨through⟩?

Clearly, the decision *whether* to translate 'element by element' or translate 'element by sequence', and *what* sequence to establish as match for an element, simply depends on the

[1] See pp. 71ff., below.

requirements of adequate translation. But whether part of a message *is* an element or *is* a sequence has to be determined entirely on evidence internal to each medium. With regard to our orthography, then, shall we regard ⟨b⟩ as a sequence ⟨l+o⟩, or ⟨E⟩ as ⟨L + ֿ⟩, and ⟨F⟩ as ⟨I + ֿ⟩, or ⟨;⟩ as ⟨.+,⟩, or ⟨qu⟩ as ⟨q + u⟩?—We seem to stipulate two conditions of being a *sequence*:

(i) some measure of divisibility,—i.e. in the case of speech, the possibility of dividing the articulation or reception of it into a number of more or less ideal successive segments; and in the case of writing, some minimal spatial interval in the row, fixed with reference to some ideal standard such as kalligraphy or print; and

(ii) mutual distributional independence of the parts, i.e. distinctive ('commutable') recurrence of every part in other environments.

It appears then that, for example ⟨q⟩, ⟨p⟩, ⟨b⟩, ⟨d⟩, ⟨F⟩, ⟨E⟩, ⟨;⟩, satisfy (ii) but do not satisfy (i); while ⟨qu⟩ satisfies (i) but not (ii) (since ⟨q⟩ never occurs without ⟨u⟩). On the other hand, ⟨o⟩, ⟨I⟩, ⟨.⟩, ⟨,⟩ do not satisfy either (i) or (ii). None of these are then sequences.

The case of ⟨qu⟩ is exceptional. It *looks* like a sequence since it covers two standard intervals, but fails to be one on account of the distributional dependence of one of the segments: ⟨q⟩ requires supplementation by ⟨u⟩ (ignoring foreign names like *Aqaba*). The element, then, is ⟨qu⟩—a single grapheme matched most frequently by the phonemic sequence /kw/.[1] Are analogous cases on the lexical level equally rare? One might think of the much cited and equally exceptional 'cranberry', when 'cran-' and 'berry' behave much like ⟨q⟩ and ⟨u⟩, respectively. This is a perfect analogy. But lexical analogies need not be as perfect as that. For as I shall try to explain in a moment, a lexical element can be distributionally dependent on another

---

[1] We may note that any portion of Russian script containing the so-called soft sign, ⟨ь⟩, does satisfy the two conditions of being a sequence, and ⟨ь⟩ does qualify as a grapheme, even though it is never matched separately by any phoneme. Its companion graphemes, however, are found to be translated separately in other sequences. If this were not the case, we should come even nearer to establishing correspondences of graphemes with distinctive phonemic features, rather than with phonemes.

without being uniquely tied to it as ⟨q⟩ is to ⟨u⟩ or 'cran-' is to 'berry'. Consequently, there are far more lexical expressions which 'look' like sequences, but are not. Shall we regard *under-* and *-stand* as independent in 'understand' because *under-* occurs also in 'underwear', 'undergrowth', and *-stand* also in 'stand', 'bystander'? Is 'understand' like the pseudo-sequence ⟨qu⟩? Or is it like the genuine sequence ⟨sh⟩?[1]

Criteria of distributional independence, i.e. of distinctive occurrence of the same element in different environments, are decisive on both levels; but they are more complex on the lexical level; necessarily so, because 'occurrence of the same' is a more complex notion in the case of a lexical unit than it is in the case of a grapheme or phoneme. While there is no doubt that the same ⟨s⟩ occurs in ⟨ship⟩ and ⟨sun⟩, also the same ⟨h⟩ in ⟨ship⟩ and ⟨hot⟩, hence, that the two are independent, ⟨sh⟩ of ⟨ship⟩ being a sequence in the same sense in which, say ⟨sk⟩ of ⟨skip⟩ is a sequence: it is, to say the least, very doubtful that the same 'under' occurs in 'understand' and 'underwear', or the same 'stand' in 'understand' and 'stand'. But if, from a lexical point of view, 'under-' and '-stand' of 'understand' are distributionally dependent on one another, then the word 'understand' is not a sequence of lexical elements, but is merely homophonous with such a sequence. To do justice to the homophony, as well as to certain limited distributional similarities (between 'stand' and 'understand'),[2] we may call the latter a 'pseudo-sequence'. Similarly, idiomatic phrases—such as *talking through* (*his*) *hat* in 'He is talking through his hat' or *pulling* (*your*) *leg* in 'He is pulling your leg' could not count as genuine lexical sequences.[3] Clearly, there can be nothing of quite the same sort on the graphemic or phonemic level. 'Homographic'

---

[1] Cp. A. McIntosh (op. cit.), p. 108f., where ⟨sh⟩ is considered to be analogous to 'understand'.

[2] E.g. *stood—understood*, but *I understand you* and not **I stand you**.

[3] For the translator, it is of course important to realise that the language itself presents him here with a pseudo-sequence. He will then realise that his translation would not necessarily gain in articulateness if he were to match the original with again a sequence or pseudo-sequence, rather than an element. It is strange and sometimes amusing to witness the misplaced ambition among some language teachers always to match idiom by idiom. They might just as well insist on translating 'pomme-de-terre' by some idiomatic sequence of three English words, rather than by 'potato'.

sequences of graphemes (or 'homophonous' sequences of phonemes) are generally nothing else than instances of the same sequence. Idioms have no exact analogue on the phonemic or graphemic level. The ⟨u⟩ of ⟨qu⟩ comes near; it might be regarded as a pseudo-grapheme and part of a pseudo-sequence.[1]

If we ask, then, why pseudo-sequences should be far more common on the lexical level than they are on the lower level of phonemes and graphemes, the answer is found by referring to the elementary difference between the two levels. For a lexical element to be distributionally independent, as part of a genuine sequence, a further condition must be satisfied, over and above recurrence of the same form in other environments. In all these environments, we must have identified not only the same form but also the same lexical value. It is independent value that we are missing in the *pull* or *leg* of 'He was pulling your leg'.[2]

[1] Homophony of the non-idiomatic kind (i.e. involving two lexical values) has perhaps some rare analogues: in the difference between 'single quote' and 'apostrophe', or between 'dash' and 'hyphen'. We are dealing here with different graphemes which overlap in the same graphs; the environment decides between them: 'apostrophe' within a word but 'single quotes' before and after words. It may be significant that these exceptional graphemes are both 'prosodic' signals which operate upon higher-level units.

[2] This is not to say that, on the phonemic or graphemic level, sequence is no problem. In English phonology, for instance, the question 'element or sequence' arises with regard to units such as /tʃ/ or /dʒ/ or with regard to so-called 'diphthongs' (cp. Martinet, *Un ou deux phonemes?*, 1939, reprinted in *Readings in Linguistics*, II, University of Chicago Press, 1966, or C. F. Hockett, *A Manual of Phonology*, 161ff. (Indiana University Publications, Baltimore, 1955).

These are not pseudo-sequences; a border-line case is not pseudo. Nor are they at all analogous to 'digraphs'. For, here, a decison (if a decision is at all worth making) could only be reached on internal evidence, and has nothing to do with translation. Only after we have established /dʒ/ as a sequence on phonological grounds, would it be possible to regard it as a 'diphone' (analogous to the 'digraph') on account, say, of its translation by ⟨j⟩ (as in ⟨jam⟩). The decision 'one or two graphemes?' depends of course on the design of the script and is therefore very largely trivial; but it is not altogether arbitrary. E.g. the practice of Czech lexicographers to use ⟨ch⟩ as a separate dictionary-rubric does not alter the fact that, in Czech orthography, ⟨ch⟩ is a graphemic sequence (cp. C. E. Bazell, op. cit., p. 361).

Moreover, though the question 'One or two graphemes?' is in itself rather trivial, and the question 'One or two phonemes?' in itself only of limited interest: yet the question 'One or two lexical elements?' is more important, and to ask further why there should be this difference in significance between analogous questions is of considerable theoretical interest.

On evidence internal to the system of writing, then, there is no reason whatever for regarding ⟨sh⟩ or ⟨th⟩ as anything but sequences. It is only translation that treats the ⟨sh⟩ of ⟨ship⟩ differently from the ⟨sk⟩ of ⟨skip⟩, and the ⟨th⟩ of ⟨thick⟩ differently from the ⟨tr⟩ of ⟨trick⟩. In English orthography, ⟨quick⟩ consists of four graphemes (qu, i, c, k), ⟨mission⟩ and ⟨through⟩ are sequences of seven, and ⟨tone⟩ is a sequence of four —the elements occurring in the order of writing or reading, from left to right. Phono-graphic translation of such English words is certainly not a global 'look and say'; but it does alternate between element–element and element–sequence translation:

⟨qu i c k, m i s s i o n, t h r o u g h, t o n e⟩
/kw ɪ k, [1] m ɪ ʃ n, θ r u, t ə ʊ n /[2]

The difficulties we encounter here are of a kind familiar to translators—correspondences such as:

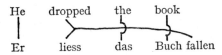

He dropped the book
Il a laissé tomber le livre

or, with discontinuous sequences:

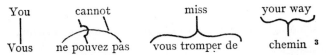

He dropped the book
Er liess das Buch fallen

You cannot miss your way
Vous ne pouvez pas vous tromper de chemin [3]

[1] For historical reasons, correspondence of a single grapheme to a sequence of phonemes (such as ⟨qu⟩—/kw/ or ⟨x⟩—/ks/) is far less common than the reverse. Almost all our bracketings are on one side. Hence, perhaps, the absence of a term 'diphone' to parallel 'digraph'.

[2] It is in the teaching of element–sequence translation that some misconceptions of the 'phonic method of teaching reading' must come to grief. Translation of a graphemic sequence into a single phoneme is not helped by reading out the constituent graphemes. (Cp. below, pp. 71ff.)

[3] A book entitled *New French Self-taught* (New York, 1952), annotates (p. 121) the English translation of this French sentence as follows: 'Literally: You *not* can *not yourself* mistake of way.' The same procedure

On the level of lexical translation, the difficulties are in fact far greater. For, the sequences to be matched by elements are practically infinite in number and variety. It would be a hopeless task to try to list them. This is why dictionaries must generally content themselves with giving translations of pseudo-sequences, i.e. of idiomatic phrases only. In phono-graphic translation, on the other hand, any graphemic sequence which is to be translated by a single phoneme may be regarded as part of a closed list of correspondences, i.e. as part of the prevailing alphabetic convention. This does not mean, however, that the operations of writing or reading will always be performed in a pre-ordained way by actually referring to such a list. No doubt this will be so in many cases; for instance, when translating ⟨sh⟩ or ⟨ph⟩ or ⟨o . . . e⟩. But frequently enough—for example, in the case of 'mission'—there is more than one way, and one may be easier than another (see below, p. 78).

4.2.2. *Distribution of the Burden of Choice*

The difficulty of translation, we have seen, consists primarily in searching for, and choosing, 'target'-units to match the 'source'. Phono-graphic translation, when it operates within a fairly 'regular' alphabetic convention (i.e. a convention which favours approximate one-to-one correspondence between phonemes and graphemes), presents to one equally familiar with both media a task which will call for about the same effort in both directions. It will be fairly simple, no matter whether the target is phonic or graphic. With an 'irregular' alphabetic convention however, the burden of choice may be distributed unevenly between the two directions of translation: the scales may be weighted in favour of either reading or writing.[1] And

---

is followed throughout the book. Surely, a precise analogy to a misconceived phonic method of teaching reading. This particular method announces itself (appropriately) as 'Practical Linguistry'. In fact, the book is better, in intention and execution, than this methodological aberration would lead one to expect. Clearly, the same problem of element-sequence matching has produced similar pedagogical blunders in phono-graphic and lexical translations.

[1] I am, of course, referring to 'reading aloud' and 'writing down'. The problems we are discussing do not exist for 'original' writing or 'silent' reading.

it is generally the case that alphabetic conventions present different problems for readers and writers.

Correspondence between phonemes and graphemes, if it is not one-to-one, can be either one-many or many-one or many-many; and which of these it is must profoundly affect the use of the alphabet, whether by readers or writers. If disjunctive correspondences *diverge towards phonemes, rather than graphemes* conversion into speech will be the more difficult; if they *diverge towards graphemes, rather than phonemes*, the difficulty will be with conversion into writing.

This is again in accord with our experience of ordinary interlingual translation. In the case of a disjunctive correspondence diverging from English to French, such as

it is more difficult to translate English into French than French into English. The task of selection is more complex when the target is French than when it is English. The reverse would be true of

In the same way, among phonographic correspondences:
(1) With those diverging towards graphemes, rather than phonemes, such as

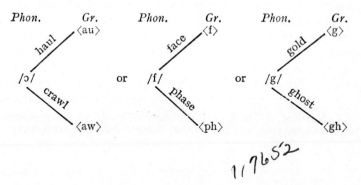

117652

it is easier to read than to write; while

(2) with those diverging towards phonemes, rather than graphemes, such as

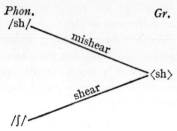

it is easier to write than to read.

Cases of a purely uni-directional divergence are few in English orthography. Most graphemes are 'polyphonic', and most phonemes are 'polygraphic'. When there is an asymmetry of effort between reading and writing, it is due to the choice being *easier* in one direction than in the other, rather than to choice being imposed on one and not on the other (cp. 4.3)

In English orthography, most correspondences between phonemes and graphemes are many-many. But it is possible for an alphabetic convention to favour one-many correspondences in one direction. French orthography, for instance, operates predominantly with divergences due to polygraphy. This is why it 'enables the foreigner to be sure of the pronunciation of a word, of which he knows the written form', while it is at the same time 'exceptionally troublesome for those who have already learned how to pronounce the language, before reading and writing it'.[1] What is troublesome for the latter—that is, especially for the French schoolchildren—is in fact just the writing. English orthography is not so biased. Being burdened, and overburdened, with both kinds of divergent correspondence, it is just as troublesome to read as it is to write.

From a social point of view, ability to read is obviously far more important than ability to write. It would therefore be reasonable if a programme of English spelling-reform were to concentrate on reducing the polyphony of graphemes, while perhaps tolerating their isophonic merging. And one might follow a similar plan when designing an introductory teaching

[1] A. Martinet, *Eléments de Linguistique Générale*, p. 165 (Collection Armand Colin, 1960, English version, Faber & Faber, London, 1964).

alphabet. Here, though, one would in this way reinforce the bias towards reading which is already present in the situation. The alphabetic script being acquired as a second language, reading must in any case be easier at first than writing—not only as we have seen, (i) because the receptive skill of *recognising* the new (as in reading) is acquired more easily than the productive skill of *realising* it (as in writing), but also (ii) because translation into the familiar speech is simpler than translation into the new script.

Sir James Pitman's 'initial teaching alphabet' has opted for thus reinforcing this bias implicit in the learner's situation. The Minister of Education, who originally gave her blessing to some such experiment, and equally all the research which later accompanied it, have been interested primarily in reading.[1] It is not surprising, therefore, that the 'initial teaching alphabet' itself has a built-in bias towards reading. Its promoters are of course aware of this. It is not so clear, however, that they have been fully aware of the fact that their revised 'alphabet' preserves some fairly considerable obstacles to the technique of writing. Sir James Pitman himself tends to regard these as trifling. 'After all,' he says, 'to allow more than one character for a single phoneme does no great harm,' whereas to allow 'a single character to represent more than its own single phoneme' would cause 'confusion' and 'continue the present intolerable burden on the child'.[2] The difference here is, in fact, one between two kinds of confusion: the first (in the French way) for the writer, the second for the reader. I.t.a. has opted for the first.

When i.t.a. preserves an *isophonic merging* of graphemes (polygraphic phonemes) such as (to cite just a few)

[1] Cp. the titles of Sir James Pitman's papers: 'Learning to Read' (1961), 'The Future of the Teaching of Reading' (1963), and the very name of that 'Reading Research Unit', which, under J. Downing, investigated the results of the i.t.a. experiment.
[2] 'Learning to Read' (1961), p. 16.

or

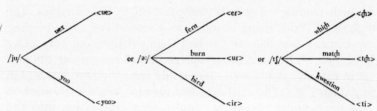

the difficulty 'reading-wise' will be slight, but the writer's choice cannot be easy. Indeed, some isophonic equivalences, which i.t.a. has *not* preserved, would seem to cause far less trouble. For example, the isophony of ⟨x⟩ and ⟨ks⟩ or of ⟨qu⟩ and ⟨kw⟩,

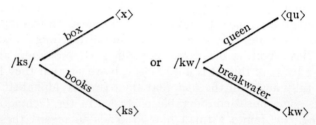

which are not admitted to i.t.a., seem to be less troublesome than, say, the competition between ⟨j⟩ and ⟨di⟩, which is accepted.

Similarly, with regard to *polyphonic splits* of graphemes (isographic merging of phonemes). It appears that Sir James Pitman has eradicated some rather innocuous polyphonies of English orthography, e.g.

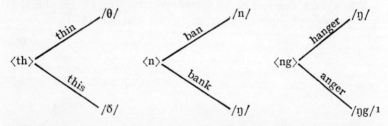

It is difficult to see why these should have been regarded as harmful—even 'reading-wise'; there is very little to be gained

<hr>

[1] The last of these distinctions is not made in some English dialects, and the absence of it does not reduce their capacity of making all the required lexical distinctions.

from writing ⟨ᵺis, baŋk, haŋer, aŋger⟩. Here, Sir James would probably appeal to a *principle*—namely the demand for unique phonemic translation. He has claimed at times that, in i.t.a., no concession has been made to polyphonic translation.[1] But this claim is not borne out by the facts. Concessions have been made; and some polyphonies which have been accepted seem to be more vexing than others (such as those just cited) which have been rejected; for example, there must be some difficulty for the reader in the correspondences

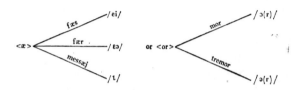

or in the ⟨u⟩ of i.t.a., which transcribes /ʌ/ (as in ⟨sum⟩) and also contributes to the transcription of /əː/ ⟨wurd⟩, /ɔ/—⟨aull⟩, /u/—⟨juesy⟩, /ju/—⟨nue⟩, /aʊ/—⟨hou⟩.

Clearly, the underlying principle of i.t.a.—its bias towards easy reading rather than writing—has not been adhered to without qualifications.[2] Yet, the point of noting this is not to complain of inconsistency—even though the claims made for the script provoke such criticism. The fault, in fact, seems to lie precisely in having aspired to the wrong kind of consistency. The idea seems to have been that the designer of an alphabet *ought* to adhere to one overriding requirement; when, in fact, what the task demanded was a balance to be struck between conflicting requirements. But if this is the case, then no one principle—such as 'elimination of polyphony'—can possibly be sufficient as a guide to orthographic revision. And if other considerations are bound to influence the designer's decisions—as they obviously did in the present case—then these considerations ought to be made explicit.

When, of the many obstacles with which the traditional

---

[1] E.g. 'Learning to Read', loc. cit.

[2] Cp. also John Mountford, 'i.t.a. as a Grading Device' (Reading Research Document No. 5. University of London Institute of Education). I am indebted to Mr. Mountford for his checking of my references to i.t.a.

orthography obstructs the writing of English, some are to remain with us while others are removed, we shall want to know by what criteria the chaff was divided from the grain. Similarly, when even some obstacles to reading are tolerated, we should be able to state exactly, what it is that is supposed to redeem them. We have been told that phono-graphic divergence (in one direction or the other) is to be conceded only if it assists a later transition to the traditional orthography. But to say this without further specification, is to say nothing at all. Since *every* revision of the orthography must make that later transition more difficult, the question remains why we should keep some of the traditional divergencies while rejecting others. It seems to be assumed that the appropriate choice of target-units (for reading or writing) is easier in some cases than it is in others. But mere assumption is not enough. This is the question we must turn to now: In the case of a prima facie problematic translation, what are the principal clues and tendencies that determine the translator's choice?[1]

4.3. Controlled Choice

4.3.1. *Types of Clues*

It is true that, taken in isolation, almost every English phoneme is polygraphic, and almost every English grapheme polyphonic. Something analogous may be said of words belonging to different languages, when considered out of context, i.e. as dictionary-citations. Technical terms excepted, almost every word in *either* of two languages contracts one-many correspondence with words in the other.[2] A list of the alternative correspondents, which an isolated word has in another language, is basically

---

[1] When these conditions of choice are carefully examined, many deviations of i.t.a. from a phonetic script will appear to be well worth having. Indeed, many more phono-graphic divergencies of English orthography will be found to be redeemed; and a revision even more limited than i.t.a., and rather on the lines proposed by Dr. Wijk, may recommend itself. However, much more research is required here. (Cp. also J. Downing, *Evaluating the Initial Teaching Alphabet*.)

[2] It would be useful to have a *general* term for this kind of translation-correspondence—a term covering the polygraphic phoneme, the polyphonic grapheme, the poly-French English word, etc.: 'polytropic' might perhaps be acceptable.

nothing else than a compilation of the various translations that would be made of it in different contexts. The word lives in context; there is an air of unreality about those lists of disjunctive correspondences—the phono-graphic lists of the orthographer no less than the lexical ones of a bilingual dictionary. What they abstract from is precisely the *conditions* which the translator must observe in making a choice from the list of items. In phono-graphic translation, many of these restrictions upon the translator's choice are more or less regular. This is often overlooked—as for example, when Bernard Shaw remarks (tongue in cheek, no doubt) that the rules of English orthography allow the pronunciation of ⟨fish⟩ to be matched equally well by ⟨ghoti⟩ (⟨gh⟩ as in ⟨tough⟩, ⟨o⟩ as in ⟨women⟩, and ⟨ti⟩ as in ⟨nation⟩. It is true that ⟨gh⟩ appears in a list of four graphemes—⟨f, ff, gh, ph⟩—all corresponding to /f/, and ⟨o⟩ appears in another list as corresponding to /ɪ/, and ⟨ti⟩ among a large number of items corresponding to /ʃ/. Nonetheless, according to the rules of English orthography ⟨fɪʃ/ *can* only be written ⟨fish⟩[1] while, conversely ⟨ghoti⟩ could not be pronounced otherwise than /gəʊtɪ/.[2]

It is because there *are* such rules for English and because on the whole they are rules for matching graphemes or grapheme—

---

[1] We find ⟨phish⟩ excluded for morpho-graphemic reasons, initial ⟨phi⟩ being almost invariably ⟨philo⟩. Even less probable would be ⟨physh⟩ or ⟨fysh⟩; ignoring proper names, the first because ⟨y⟩ does not seem to occur before ⟨sh⟩, and the second, furthermore, because it does not occur after initial ⟨f⟩.

[2] Lists of graphemes corresponding to the various English phonemes are found in R. A. Hall's *Sound and Spelling in English*. For the other part of an English phono-graphic 'dictionary' we have to turn to another book (which itself lacks the first part)—namely, A. Wijk's *Rules of Pronunciation for the English Language*. The latter gives us also rules by which context determines the translation of graphemes into speech. Hall's lists are, in fact, useful only, if taken in conjunction with Wijk's treatment. By themselves, even in conjunction with a very sketchy list of 'regular graphemic representations', they give a distorted picture of the relevant relations. It is misleading, for instance, when phoneme /ɪ/ is said to be 'represented' by the English graphemes ⟨i, ie, e, o, u, y, ui⟩, without its being made clear (with the help of a survey such as Wijk's) that /ɪ/ is translated ⟨o⟩ only in *women*, and (in a stressed syllable) ⟨u⟩ only in *busy*, ⟨ui⟩ only in *build* (and its derivatives), ⟨ie⟩ only in *sieve*, ⟨e⟩ only in *England, English, pretty*—which leaves, in fact, for the many thousands of occurrences of the English phoneme /ɪ/, only ⟨i⟩ and ⟨y⟩ to be sorted out by phono-graphic rules.

sequences with *phonemes*, that the English system of writing, though not 'phonetic', is still basically alphabetic.

For a system of writing to be alphabetic it is not necessary that the rules for translation of phonemes should refer only to phonological, or low-level graphemic, conditions. What any such rule refers to is the *context* in which the phonemes occur; and contextual conditions may be referred to outside of phonological or graphemic terms. If, for instance, we say '⟨ti⟩ always /ʃ/ in words ending in ⟨-tion⟩' ('nation', 'definition', 'action', etc.), we are stating a restriction on the choice of target phonemes, though expressing it in *grammatical* terms.

We may say generally of *any* kind of translation that the conditions which determine the choice of target-units are distinguishable as either 'same level' or 'higher level'. Thus, the restrictions upon a translator's choice of *lexical* units are either (i) 'syntactic-collocational' (if they refer to neighbouring lexical units) or (ii) 'stylistic' (if they refer to the wider context of discourse).

It is, for example, a syntactic rule (operating upon lexical elements within the limits of the sentence) that requires 'know' to be translated by French 'connais' in the context 'I know Paul', and by 'sais' in the context 'I know nothing'.[1] Similarly the choice between German *wenn* and *als* as alternative translations of English *when* is often syntactically conditioned: for example, in 'When he asks for information . . .', where the present tense of *asks* compels translation by *wenn*. On the other hand, only higher-level ('stylistic') considerations can tell us how to translate *when* in 'When he asked for information, I gave it'. We have to decide here whether in the wider context it would be appropriate to replace *when* by *whenever*, in which case we choose *wenn*,—otherwise *als*. The decision is still easy enough; but it is not nearly so clear-cut as in the other cases: in rejecting *Als er fragt. . . .* or **Je sais Paul*, we excluded the impossible, whereas now we would be excluding the less appropriate. There can be explicit rules against the impossible but hardly for defining and choosing what is more appropriate. The general

---

[1] On this English-to-French divergence, cp. A. McIntosh 'A four-letter word in *Lady Chatterley's Lover*' (1960), which examines 'the extent to which grammatical as distinct from collocational (lexical) criteria are adequate for the solution of problems of this kind'. (In McIntosh and Halliday, *Patterns of Language*, Longmans, 1966.)

procedure, however, of finding guidance for our choice of target-units is the same in both cases; we examine the *contextual conditions* of the particular source-units. It is generally the case that *lexical* choice requires us to consult contexts wider than the sentence: i.e. our criteria for choosing among the prima facie alternatives are generally 'stylistic'. It may take a very long stretch of text (perhaps even external information) to discover whether, let us say, the German *Nebel* should be turned into English by *haze* or *mist* or *fog*.

Let us note that, unlike interlingual translation, phono-graphic translation generally works to a standard: it chooses the 'correct', and eliminates the 'incorrect'. This, however, is but a consequence of the fact that a closed set of settled correspondences can easily enumerate all phonographic translations.[1] The operations, however, remain basically the same. The problems of having to choose among alternative correspondences are similar; and the restrictions which govern and lighten the translator's burden of choice are of the same two kinds: namely—(i) 'same level', i.e. 'phonotactic' or 'grapho-tactic' (belonging, as it were, to the syntax of phonemes or graphemes) and (ii) 'higher level', i.e. 'morpho-phonemic' or 'morpho-graphemic'.

To illustrate: If we say (with certain qualifications) 'Grapheme ⟨c⟩ sounds /k/ if it occurs before ⟨a, o, u⟩, but /s/ before ⟨e, i, y⟩', we are referring to purely graphemic conditions of the occurrence of ⟨c⟩; we are stating a *graphotactic* rule for the *reader*. Similarly, when we say (in the other direction) 'phoneme /k/, initially in a stressed syllable, is generally written ⟨k⟩ before /i, ɪ, e/, but ⟨c⟩ before other phonemes', we are stating a *phonotactic* rule for the *writer*.

On the other hand, it is a *morpho-graphemic* rule that directs the reader to match ⟨tear⟩ in some contexts ('shedding . . .' etc.), with /tɪə/, and in others (' . . . off', ' . . . the paper', etc.) with /tɛə/. And it is a *morpho-phonemic* rule that settles whether /veɪn/ is to be written ⟨vein⟩ or ⟨vain⟩, or ⟨vane⟩. More precisely, in any particular case, the decision—as between ⟨ei⟩, ⟨ai⟩, and ⟨a . . e⟩, to match /eɪ/—is clearly not made by

---

[1] It is because interlingual translation-correspondences are not so surveyable that they are incapable of being laid down in a 'code of rules'. This is *the* obstacle to mechanical translation.

reference to the latter's phonemic environment; the writer's choice is determined by the lexical (morphemic) value of the whole sequence /vein/ in the utterance in which it occurs.[1] In some cases, logographic or logophonic considerations *supplement* a basically alphabetic convention.

If we ask about a translator's *ease* in choosing amongst more or less *regular* correspondences, we find that this varies from case to case. Broadly, the motives in favour of some particular 'target', seem to be of two kinds: some concern the target itself, others concern the contextual conditions in which it is appropriate. The first (*tendencies*) have to do with the kind of regularity which is founded on *frequency*, the second with regularity founded on *general rule*. We shall examine these two (4.3.2 and 4.3.3), before turning to the truly irregular logographic or logophonic conventions (4.3.4).

4.3.2. *Tendencies*

Tendencies have been given a good deal of attention. The sheer frequency of the occasions on which some particular translation has been chosen is certainly significant in establishing a general tendency to it. In Dr. Wijk's *Regularized English*, this has been the main consideration for establishing the regularities of the English orthography. He preserves, for instance, the graphemic ⟨ear⟩ where it reads /ɪə/, but replaces it ('regularizes' it) where it reads /ɛə/. One should then continue to shed a ⟨tear⟩, but should ⟨tair⟩ one's hair; the reason being that the /ɛə/ translation applies in fact to only six English words.

It will be important here to agree on what is to be measured. When some particular translation (i.e. some particular correspondence) is said to 'predominate', we shall have to ask what exactly is to be counted as 'dominance'—whether just the number, in the language, of different words to which it applies, or also the relative frequency, in use, of these words. To put it briefly: Do we determine 'dominance' by *'lexical incidence'*

---

[1] The exclusion of ⟨ey⟩ and ⟨ay⟩, on the other hand, seems to be possible simply by reference to the non-final occurrence of /eɪ/ in /veɪn/. (Exceptions like ⟨always⟩ seem to be very few). And no decision at all is required for excluding ⟨au⟩ of 'gauge' or ⟨ea⟩ of 'great'. These are not even candidates for choice, though they are listed with the others in the usual compilations of phono-graphic divergencies (as in R. A. Hall, op. cit., p. 30).

only, or by *overall frequency*?[1] Many of the most common words of English—'you', 'could', 'would', 'have', 'give', 'come', 'great', etc., etc.,—will have to be regarded as exceptional in their spelling (their phono-graphic correspondence being dubbed irregular), if 'exceptional' has been defined in terms of incidence, i.e. as 'applicable to relatively few *words*'; but they would have to be rated as normal ('regular') in spelling, if 'exceptional' ('irregular') has been defined in terms of overall frequency, i.e. as 'applicable to relatively few *word-occurrences*'.

Dr. Wijk makes a clear distinction between these two measures. When he asks about reading-facility (and he is not really concerned with writing), he assesses the comparative regularity of *any particular phono-graphic correspondence* in terms of incidence. Of the different readings of a grapheme, he asks which applies to the largest number of different words in the language. But having determined in this way, which words are pronounced regularly, he then estimates the regularity of *the script as a whole* by applying both measures: the words of *irregular* spelling are counted as a percentage, not only of the number of vocabulary items, but also of the number of words on an average page.[2] The two percentages are not the same for English: only the second takes account of frequency of actual occurrence. The irregular common words crowd any piece of continuous writing to such an extent as to swell its irregularity to 30 per cent of the words per page, while of the words in a dictionary no more than 10 per cent are irregular.[3]

The most common English words, then, present a problem for spelling-reform proposals. It is tempting to exclude them from revision, and so to reduce the gap between the reformed and the traditional script by no less than two-thirds. There seems to be some hesitation, here. But even the 'Simplified Spelling Society' has found it possible to relax its principles for the sake of 'the most frequently recurring words', and to admit

[1] 'Incidence' is a useful term introduced by W. G. Moulton in his comparative study of dialects (e.g. *The short vowel systems of Northern Switzerland*, WORD, 16.2, 1960).

[2] Strictly speaking, the percentages, being obtained for *words*, would have to be multiplied to give us percentages for irregular grapheme–phoneme translation. For, in very many cases, one word contains more than one irregular grapheme–phoneme correspondence.

[3] See Vol. I, *Alphabets for English*, Wijk, pp. 53, 73.

them with a spelling which by those principles is 'irregular'.[1] I.t.a. has gone back on such concessions, though content to grant others (such as the divergent spellings of /ə/ in 'sister, actor, beggar'). Dr. Wijk, on the other hand, for whom those common words are in any case less 'irregular', has also been more generous with his concessions to 'continuity' and 'less disturbance'. However, with regard to all these 'concessions', it is never really clear why the reasons which are given for making them in some cases should not equally apply to others where concessions have been refused.

The two interpretations of frequency allow us to argue either way. We may say that the low incidence of a 'spelling' in *just a few* common words condemns it; but also that high overall frequency in a few *common* words sanctions it. From a psychological point of view, it may be claimed that the irregular spelling of just a few words is harmless—for one can easily remember the few exceptions; but also, that a phono-graphic convention is grasped most readily through constant exemplification in the most common words, which means that irregularity in these must be harmful. Such uncertainty makes it only more important to realise that arguments from frequency are not *sufficient* to establish the regularity of any particular 'spelling'. The reader's or writer's choice of a phono-graphic translation is also determined by other factors. Not that these have escaped all notice but they do not seem, so far, to have received the attention they deserve.[2]

4.3.3. *Rules.*

Our inclination, on any particular occasion, to translate a text in one way rather than another may be due not only to the

[1] See Vol. I, P. A. D. MacCarthy, pp. 100, 103. The American 'Simpler Spelling Association' has argued recently that the ⟨th⟩—/ð/ correspondence should be regarded as more prominent (or regular) than ⟨th⟩—/θ/, because its overall frequency is far greater, though its lexical incidence is much less (Papers circulated July, 1967).

[2] Dr. Wijk states: 'The statistical relationship between the different uses of a certain symbol should not be the only criterion . . . in determining which uses should be retained and which should be discarded in Regularized English. Due regard should also be paid to the conformity of the various uses to the general orthographic structure of the language.' (*Regularized English*, p. 92.) What seems wanted is some clearer exposition of what is here referred to as 'general orthographic structure of the language'.

frequency of the chosen match itself but also to the force with which its context demands it, or indeed, to both, We have seen that there are two kinds of contextual condition: 'same level' and 'higher level'. We are asking now about the force with which either of these may 'condition' us to prefer a certain translation. When circumstances or conditions of an operation are taken account of in this way, they are generally referred to in terms of *rules*. Any descriptive statement of a *regularity* such as: '$\langle c \rangle$ before $\langle e \rangle$, $\langle i \rangle$, $\langle y \rangle$ *is* read /s/' may be formulated as a *rule* (a rule for the translator) '$\langle c \rangle$ before $\langle e \rangle$, $\langle i \rangle$, $\langle y \rangle$ *to be* read /s/'.

Among rules, some are 'stronger', easier to comply with, than others. This relative strength of a rule seems to depend on its comparative *simplicity* and *generality*. Put more exactly: the force of a rule can be measured by the comparative simplicity and generality of the *description* we may give *of the conditions* in which it operates—a description such as 'before $\langle e \rangle$, $\langle i \rangle$, $\langle y \rangle$'.[1] Other things being equal, we tend to translate by the simplest rule, and also by the most general rule.

Contextual Rules.— How *simplicity* helps may be illustrated easily with reference to graphotactic rules. Those, for instance, which require an English 'vowel-letter' (so-called) to be read 'long' (as in *go, tone, noble*), differ greatly in relative complexity: of the descriptions of the relevant conditions, (1) 'in word-final position' (as for *go*) is simpler than (2) 'before a consonant-letter plus silent $\langle e \rangle$' (as for *tone*); and this is simpler than (3) 'before a consonant-letter plus $\langle l \rangle$ or $\langle r \rangle$ plus silent $\langle e \rangle$' (as for *noble*).[2] This will remain true, even if we do not forget, that the configurational recognition of complex conditions is always much simpler than any analytic description of them may suggest.

Simplicity of a rule is often reinforced by *generality*. Some of

[1] This means that any more precise application of the terms 'simple' and 'general' would need to refer to the whole framework of linguistic description—something that would go beyond the scope even of this steadily expanding study. However, our use of the two terms is not difficult to illustrate. At the same time, it is interesting to note that apparently *formal* characteristics of a 'mere' *description*, such as its simplicity and generality, are indicative of *effective forces* in the described situation itself: so much so that we are inclined to speak inappropriately of simple or general *conditions*, when in fact we are referring to simple or general *descriptions* of them.

[2] It should be noted that the phonological structure of English excludes translation of final $\langle e \rangle$ by /e/. See below, 72f.

the contextual conditions which guide the translator's choice are easy to take account of, because the category they belong to is so general as to be exemplified in *every* translation. Thus, to describe the occurrence of a grapheme as 'initial', 'medial' or 'final' with regard to a morpheme, word, or sentence, is to characterise it by a kind of condition, recognition of which is essential to graphemic or phonemic analysis. It is then also on account of its categorial generality, that condition (1) above ('word-final') is so easy to observe. For the same reason, we shall find it fairly easy to choose, say, between the two principal pronunciations of the English digraph ⟨ie⟩—namely, (1) within a morpheme, as in 'believe, chief, field', where it is translated /i/, and (2) morpheme-final, as in 'die, dies, cried, pies', where it is translated /aɪ/.[1] For a child to respond to these conditions, and to resolve the polyphony of ⟨ie⟩, it need only perceive that ⟨chie + f⟩ or ⟨fie + ld⟩ is somehow very different from ⟨die + d⟩ or ⟨pie + s⟩. He is, of course, not required to master the linguistic terms which help us to sort out such cases and to predict his responses.

Frequently, grammatical conditions of a somewhat lower degree of generality are yet found to be sufficiently prominent and well-defined to ensure correct choices in reading aloud. Native speakers of English find no difficulty in reading the polyphonic ⟨s⟩ in 'cats, cows, horses' or in 'Jack's, Paul's, James's' or in 'he walks, goes, dances'. In all these positions, ⟨s⟩ is retained by Dr. Wijk on what might be called 'morpho-graphemic' grounds. The same reasons could, I think, be cited for retaining ⟨s⟩ in 'is, has, does, says', and even 'was', also in 'his, hers, ours, yours, theirs', where Dr. Wijk has decided for regularising ⟨s⟩ to ⟨z⟩.[2] Similar is the case of ⟨d⟩ or ⟨ed⟩ in, say, 'lived, waited, wished'; one would not expect this polyphony to present any special difficulty for readers of English.[3]

---

[1] This is Dr. Wijk's reason for keeping ⟨ie⟩ in both cases.

[2] It seems that Dr. Wijk has here been guided by an altogether too narrow notion of 'suffix', where, in fact, a reader's responses would be to a phonological 'marker' of a grammatical category—the same marker in 'has' and 'goes', and also the same in 'his' and 'Paul's'. (Cp. *Regularized English*, p. 286.) See also below, p. 77, n. 2.

[3] 'Regularized English' writes ⟨wisht⟩.—There is, of course, another difficulty here—namely, that of choosing between ⟨i..e⟩ and ⟨-ed⟩. Writing, too, seems to be a little more difficult here—probably because of 'learnt, sent, spelt, etc.' and adjectivals like 'blessed, wretched'.

Another example is the reading of ⟨th⟩ as/ð/, rather than /θ/, in word-initial position. It will be adequately motivated by regular correlation with a fairly well defined category of words— in this case, a semantic rather than a grammatical category. Only 'than' and 'though' fail to have the peculiar deictic connotation of English words beginning /ð–/ most of which are very frequent.[1]

In the cases just cited, rules referring to *morphographemic* conditions instruct the *reader* how to resolve the *polyphony* of certain graphemes. Similarly, rules referring to *morphophonemic* conditions will frequently tell the *writer* how to resolve the *polygraphy* of phonemes. A prominent example in English is the multiple polygraphy of the so-called 'murmur vowel' /ə/ or of the syllabicity of /l̩/ and /n̩/, which may correspond to almost any 'vowel-letter' and to many sequences of such.

The *reading* of the letters corresponding to /ə/ or to syllabic /l̩/, /n̩/ causes very little difficulty to native speakers of English; they merely need to supply the appropriate and familiar stress-pattern in order to read ⟨a, e, i, o, u, ou, ai,⟩ etc. in 'leg*a*l, reb*e*l, civ*i*l, symb*o*l, caref*u*l, cauti*ou*s, mount*ai*n,' etc.— all as /ə/. And a foreigner, though at a disadvantage, could easily be helped by the provision of accentual marks to select correctly the different vowel readings in 'leg*a*l,—leg*a*lity, civ*i*l—civ*i*lity, symb*o*l—symb*o*lic', etc. The ease of these distinctions, 'reading-wise', has disposed many orthographers, who (like Sir James Pitman or Dr. Wijk) accept a bias for reading, to ignore the considerable difficulties which this polygraphy presents to the writer of English—and especially to the English writer. The European foreigner will be better off with phonographic translation in this direction. Many of the words

---

[1] A number of tests conducted by Mr. Jim Chandley and Mr. Kenneth James in schools in the Manchester area, have confirmed many such expectations. With regard to the noun plural or 3rd sg. ⟨-s⟩, orthographic mistakes were found almost exclusively among those English children who had learned to read through the i.t.a. script which is unnecessarily 'phonetic' at this point (⟨cats, caus, horsis⟩).—It has become evident that the general neglect of *grammatical* motives for 'corect' reading and writing is a major failing of most deliberations on alphabetic reform. Dr. Wijk, having abandoned the ideal of phonetic transcription, seems to be the only writer in this field to refer occasionally to grammatical conditions of grapheme occurrences.

involved belong to a common Latin-European stock, and reference to French, German or Russian will often help the foreign
learner of English to choose the letters which, in any particular
case, correspond to /ə/ or /l̩/ or /n̩/.

However, even the monoglot English writer is not entirely
without clues. If he were, his spelling would be far more erratic.
Yet the clues he makes use of, without being able to specify
them, do not seem to have been sorted out. And this neglect is
due, not only to the reading-bias of many orthographers, but to
the *phonetic* bias of practically all who have concerned themselves with problems of reading and writing. The clues which
are in fact taken account of, when /ə/ or /l̩/ or /n̩/ are written,
are very largely higher-level conditions of the occurrence of
these phonemes.

For example:—The translation of /-əl/ and /-l̩/ by ⟨-el⟩ or
⟨-ol⟩ or ⟨-il⟩ seems to occur mainly with (1) simple (underived)
nouns ('barrel, shovel, symbol, petrol, peril, council', etc.) On
the other hand (2) de-verbal derived nouns ('refusal, rehearsal,
recital, approval', etc.) require translation of /əl/ or /l̩/ into
⟨-al⟩. So do (3) de-nominal adjectives ('herbal, tribal, global,
bridal, fatal', etc.) Again (4) derived or inflected verbal forms
generally require /-ən/, /n̩/ to be written ⟨-en⟩ (cp. 'fasten,
loosen, ripen, deepen; eaten, taken', etc.) This particular
correspondence covers also most verbs and adjectives in /-ən/,
('listen, happen; open, golden, flaxen, even') and many nouns
('garden, kitchen, heaven, dozen'); while the translation /-ən/,
/n̩/→⟨-on⟩ is restricted almost exclusively to (5) words which
are, at least potentially, nouns ('person, cotton, bacon, Briton,
nation, occasion', etc.).

Each of these rules is simple and fairly general, but there are
many more of them; the ones just cited merely seemed to
offer themselves at a first glance. A proper sorting out of the
relevant rules (correspondence-regularities) would be quite a
formidable task—simply on account of the mass of words to be
surveyed. But it would seem to be worthwhile. To doubt this
on the ground that writers of English could not possibly be
credited with a power of 'observing' so many different conditions would be like doubting that a speaker of English could be
credited with observing the many regularities of English
grammar. It is true, of course, that in one sense he does not

know them; but it is also true that he knows how to comply with them. Let us note, too, that the amount of grammatical information required for the use of the English orthography varies from case to case (cp. p. 68, n. 1).

It may well turn out that the relatively few cases in which writers of English persist in being uncertain of their spelling are precisely such as fall outside any more general rules; while, on the other hand, unproblematic spellings are either individually frequent or according to rule. This assumption is plausible, and worth testing.[1] Writers of English seem to find it fairly easy to distinguish the two kinds of /braɪdl/ in 'a bridal gown' and 'horse's bridle' (cp. (3)); while, on the other hand, there tends to be persistent uncertainty about 'principal' and 'principle'. We seem to be surer about 'soften' or 'moisten' (4) than about 'beckon' or 'blazon' (which are against (5)). We have no doubt about 'survival' (2), but might hesitate about 'vassal' or 'offal' (for which there is no rule) or about 'unravel' or 'dishevel' (which offend against (1)). Again, there is uncertainty about the alternative versions of /əbl/ and /-ənt/ in 'distant— insistent, dependent—concordant, contemptible—translatable', which do not follow any general rule of English grammar.

If assumptions like these, which would be suggested by an explicit statement of correspondence-regularities, were tested and confirmed, then, we should have a basis for a number of carefully selected reform-proposals. And these would have a fair chance of being accepted, for to act upon them would merely serve to remove prevailing fluctuations of spelling, in the way in which uncertainty about ⟨-ise⟩ and ⟨-ize⟩ is being resolved at present in favour of ⟨-ise⟩.

Transformation Rules.— There is one further point of more general significance to be noted about the present example of controlled choice. It may illustrate the importance of a contextual clue which transgresses the *given* contextual conditions. Some of the 'transcription'-rules mentioned above contain such descriptive phrases as 'de-verbal nouns', 'de-nominal adjectives', 'derived verbal forms', which clearly refer to something beyond

---

[1] These problems of general orthographic structure have not been touched even by those classifications of spelling-errors which, like Mr. Spache's (op. cit., pp. 129ff.), try to separate 'unphonetic' from 'phonetically reasonable' errors.

the translated item and its actual context. When we characterise the noun 'refusal' as derived, we are referring to some other item 'refuse', which occurs in other contexts but is related to the translated 'refusal'; the two are related in the grammatical *system of the language*, not in any given utterance. Such relations —transformational relations—have been given special attention recently in 'generative' grammatical studies; but they have of course always been prominent in our traditional grammars. Whenever orthographers or spelling reformers have argued for accepting the polygraphy of the 'reduced' or 'neutral' vowel, they have defended its various graphic representations as a means of marking 'closely related words'.[1] This facility is felt to be a special advantage of *written* English. It is not without a certain informative value to write '*Satan*' and '*satanic*' instead of /seɪtən/ and /sətænɪk/, or '*total*' and '*total*ity' instead of /təʊtl/ and /təʊtælɪtɪ/. Systematic transform-relations, of a

[1] See, for instance, A. Wijk, *Regularized English*, p. 212. Also I. J. Pitman, *Learning to Read*, p. 19, and P. MacCarty, p. 103f. in Vol. I.

A generative derivation of phonetic representations (such as presented, for instance, in *The Sound Pattern of English*) is of course highly interesting in its own right. It tells us *how little* there is left for lower-level regularities to contribute towards a phonetic representation of any utterance when the syntactic structure ('surface structure') of the sentence and the morphological structure of words (including their inflectional and derivational relations) are always assumed to be known, as 'underlying' the operation of supervening 'lower-level' rules. But a generative model of the proposed kind cannot tell us *how much* can be accounted for in terms of lower-level regularities (or rules), and to what extent our linguistic operations depend on *varying amounts of grammatical information*. This may be of little significance for the construction of a model of 'linguistic competence'; but it is highly important for exploring problems of linguistic *performance*, such as those of phonographic translation.

Here, we cannot even ask the significant questions without *ordering* the prevailing regularities of correspondence: that is, ordering the rules for translation according to the amount of grammatical information that is required for them to operate. This varying amount—from the low-level generalisations of phonemic analysis to various contextual and transformational clues—determines not only the simplicity of the rules but also the comparative ease or difficulty with which one acquires and uses an orthography. This, at any rate, seems to be a reasonable hypothesis about the operations involved, and about the comparative ease of their performance. (See also below, p. 77, n.1. Some of the relevant theoretical issues are discussed in W. Haas, 'Grammatical Prerequisites of Phonological Analysis' in J. Hamm (ed.), *Phonologie der Gegenwart*, Böhlaus Nachf., 1967.)

given item and context to others, provide us here with rules for resolving the polygraphy of /ə/, /l̩/, /ŋ/ and the polyphony of the various vowel-letters.

Awareness of such transformations might help us with the spelling of simple root words like 'metal, rebel, idyll, symbol, mental, moral'. We can refer to transformations like 'met*a*llic, reb*e*llious, id*y*llic, symb*o*lic, ment*a*lity, mor*a*lity' to provide the clue for the appropriate graphemic translation of /l̩/. We learn to become sensitive to the advantage of marking these 'paradigmatic' relations, and therefore *not* to write what we hear (that is, not *metl̩, *rebl̩, *symbl̩, etc.). There are many hundreds of such sets: victor—vict*o*rious, idiot—idi*o*tic, regular—regul*a*rity, l*u*xury—lux*u*rious, organ—org*a*nic, *a*ccident—acci*de*ntal, ped*a*nt—ped*a*ntic, d*e*mon—dem*o*nic, m*y*stery—myst*er*ious, ph*o*tograph—phot*o*graphy—photogr*a*phic, etc. The rule is very general and simple: it requires us to collect the 'full' vowels from any member of such a set, and to write them in every case. We assume (and tests would probably confirm it) that writers of English, who have such paradigms at their disposal, are making use of such paradigmatic clues.[1]

When all the rules have been accounted for, and also all tendencies (such as /-l̩/ → ⟨-al⟩ for adjectives) allowed for, there will still be very many translations (of, for example, /ə/, /l̩/, /ŋ/) which remain 'arbitrary'. 'Cattle, chattel, morsel, pencil, parcel, carol, barrel, evil; raisin, curtain; anchor, vigour'—to cite just a few—seem each to require an individual choice of 'vowel-letter'. There are even cases where the correct translation *infringes* a rule. A child writing 'nobil' or 'gentil' would have to be corrected, but ought to be credited with genuine linguistic insight. There is not much to be said for the variety of the many truly irregular, i.e. logographic and logophonic, spellings of English orthography (see below, 4.3.4). Some day, we might try to reduce their number, as the Americans have already begun to do in the case of 'vigour, labour', etc. But so long as the *regularities*, though actually observed and relied upon in many hundreds of cases, have not been sorted out, any reform-proposal would be premature.

[1] Spelling-reform is liable to disturb these rules. Sir James Pitman, for instance, keeps only some of them. He will probably write ⟨mystɛɛrius⟩ and ⟨mystery⟩, ⟨lugzωrius⟩ and ⟨lukʃhury⟩.

Lexical Analogies.— The various kinds of writer's or reader's clues so far mentioned can all be found to operate in interlingual translation. We need only remind ourselves of them to recognise them at once as familiar.

There are, for example, the many cases where different conditioned or suppletive variants of a morpheme have all the same translation into another language. As 'his, Jack's, Jones's' ask for the same ⟨-s⟩, so the English 'must' and 'had to' ask for a form of the same French 'falloir' or of the same 'müssen' in German. In either case, we are referring to contextual (distributional) values of the items to be translated.

Reference to higher-rank or higher-level conditions is, as we have seen, frequently required in order to decide between alternative translations: e.g. English *before* to be rendered by German *bevor* if it is initial in a subordinate clause, but otherwise either by *vor* (when it is preposition in a prepositional phrase) or by *vorher* (when adverb in a verbal phrase).

Transformations, too, serve often as a clue in deciding between alternative lexical correspondents. When, for example, different translations are chosen for English 'dis-' in 'dissatisfied' and 'disappointed', the reason is, clearly, that the negative transformation of the first is absent from the second. Again for some languages, different translations are required for 'were' in 'The police were armed', according to whether the sentence is, or is not, to be treated as a passive transform of 'They armed the police'. (If it is such a transform, German requires *wurde*; if not, *war*.)

It is also true that, other things being equal, the translator's facility depends on whether the conditions which determine his choice are specific (like 'past tense of *must*' or '*dis-* of disappointed') or more general (like 'initial in a subordinate clause' or 'negation'). And in either case it will be significant whether the translated item, and hence its translation, is fairly frequent or not.

Digraphs and Diphones.— The same considerations of simplicity and generality will be found to have a useful application to rules which refer to 'digraphs' (or 'diphones'), i.e. rules, here, not for choosing between alternative elements, but for deciding whether to translate by an element or a sequence (cp. 4.2.1 above). The reason why it is easy to choose between ⟨x⟩ and ⟨ks⟩ in writing

/ks/, or to choose between /θ or ð/ and /th/ in reading and sounding ⟨th⟩ is that the rule is very simple and general: the decision requires reference only to the presence or absence of morphemic boundaries. The same is true of ⟨sh⟩ and ⟨ph⟩ and of initial ⟨kn⟩ or ⟨gh⟩ and others.[1]

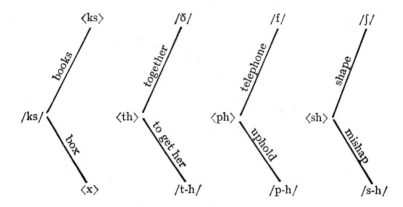

It is of course assumed that as we do not listen on the phonological level only, so we do not read only on the graphemic level. Some trial and error will be unavoidable in the case of an unskilled reader; before reading *mis+hap* and *dis+heartened*, he may have to discover that there is no morphemic sequence *mi+shap* or *dish+eartened*. But the point is that the facts are there for him to discover.

Moreover, it is true of all the 'digraphs' here that, *within* a morpheme, phonemic translation by sequence, i.e. by /th/ or /ph/ or /sh/, is excluded by the very rules of English phonology; in much the same way as translation of, say, the German morpheme-sequence *Königin* by *kingess* is excluded by the rules of English morphology. But, clearly, the fact that they are not to be translated by sequences does not prevent *Königin* or ⟨th⟩ or ⟨sh⟩ from being each a sequence of two units in its own

[1] Complex Latin words ('exit, expect, express', etc.) are obviously borrowed as morphologically simple.

Inevitably, there are borderline cases, where we are uncertain about the morphemic structure and hence possibly about the reading. Is a 'penthouse' a kind of house, and a 'loophole' a kind of hole? Some proper names which look like exceptions are cases where the sense of a morphemic boundary is disappearing or has disappeared: Petersham, Lewisham, Horsham, Carshalton, etc.

medium. For, obviously, the rules of *graphemics* do *not* exclude those sequences within morphemic boundaries, just as the rules of *German* morphology do not exclude the sequence *König* + *in* within lexical boundaries. The presence or absence of a 'higher' (morphemic or lexical) boundary only tells us how to *translate* the units concerned. Thus, analogously to the alternative translations of ⟨th⟩, ⟨sh⟩, etc.:

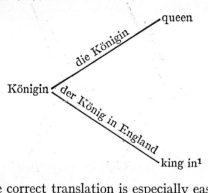

Here, too, the correct translation is especially easy to discover because the only alternative to it in the given position is a nonce-form, such as /phəʊn/ or /sheɪp/–namely, *kingess.

There are then two reasons why many of the common English digraphs are harmless: firstly, because in their own medium the necessary distinctions are made by the presence or absence of grammatical boundaries, which is enough to decide between translation by element and translation by sequence; and secondly, because rivals for the monophonemic translation are excluded by the phonological structure of English. In other words: once the morphological boundaries are noted, there can be only one pronunciation.

In spite of everything that has been said against the English digraphs, there is surely a great deal to admire in the circumspection of their originators. Indeed, there is more still to be

---

[1] The fact that the spoken morpheme *König* appears in two variants (/-ig/ and /-ix/) is of no relevance here. But there is this difference between the two cases: that the *in* of *Königin* is not 'the same' as the *in* of *der König in England*; while the same ⟨s⟩ occurs in *shape* and *mishap*. But this difference is simply due to the difference of level between the units translated in the two cases. Analogues to homophony or homography are necessarily very rare on the phonemic and graphemic levels (cp. 47f., above).

said in favour of some of them. The very nonce-form which they suggest, and which is rejected by the target-language, is not always entirely lost on us: it provides some information as to the nature of just that single phoneme which is the correct translation. In much the same way in which the rejected loan-translation *king-ess* provides us with a semantic clue to the correct *queen*, or the translation of *Handschuh* by **hand-shoe* suggests *glove*: so the rejected 'loan-translation' /p/ + /h/ at the beginning of a word surely provides a phonological clue to /f/ as a voiceless labial (like /p/) and a fricative (like /h/), as does /t/ + /h/ to the dental fricatives /θ/ and /ð/, and /s/ + /h/ to the 'wider' sibilant /ʃ/. The same was true once of the original translation of the digraph ⟨gh⟩ as in 'light, laugh', and is still true of German or Scottish ⟨ch⟩ (as in 'loch'), where /g/ (or /k/) + /h/ would clearly suggest the velar fricative. Supervening phonetic changes have here spoilt the original work of the alphabet-makers.[1]

There is less, and sometimes nothing, to be said in favour of those digraphs which are read by treating one portion of the phonologically impossible loan-translation as redundant. Examples are ⟨gh⟩ in 'ghoul, ghost', ⟨sc⟩ in 'scene, sceptre, scent', ⟨ck⟩ and ⟨ch⟩ in 'back, sick, school', or ⟨kn⟩ in 'knee, knife', etc., where ⟨h⟩ or ⟨c⟩ or ⟨k⟩ have to be ignored by the translator;[2] in much the same way as, say, in translating

---

[1] The reasons why the digraph ⟨gh⟩ presents far greater difficulties than, say, ⟨th⟩ or ⟨sh⟩ are complex: (1) The polyphony of ⟨gh⟩ does not present the translator with that simple phonemic choice between element and sequence; here, the principal alternatives are /g/ (as in 'ghost, burgher'), /f/ (as in 'laugh, tough'), and a large number of vowels ('sigh, weight, daughter, through', etc.) (2) with the exception of ⟨igh⟩ and initial ⟨gh⟩ a statement of the conditions for the various translations would be extremely complex, and would have to be specific to the extent of requiring a plain enumeration of individual cases; (3) none of the translations are favoured by special frequency; (4) the appropriate translations (again with the exception of /g/) can find no clue in the loan-translation /g/ + /h/. It should be clear that a spelling-reformer who would merely ask in a general way whether digraphs are desirable or not, and then treat ⟨th⟩ and ⟨sh⟩ in the same way as ⟨gh⟩, could only arrive at a very crude picture of English orthography, and hence at very inadequate decisions about reforming it.

[2] There is, of course, no digraph in 'Scot' or 'scoop', and the ⟨h⟩ in 'chemist, architect', etc., cannot be treated as redundant, nor is there any general rule for reading ⟨ch⟩ as /k/ in these cases. Where ⟨sc⟩ reads /s/ and ⟨ck⟩ reads /k/, the question may arise, which of the two

English negations such as 'does not come' or 'did not come' one would in most languages ignore the 'do' (though not the marker of tense).

Historically, most of the graphemes which correspond to phonological zero are fossils from an earlier period (e.g. ⟨k⟩ in *knee, knight*) and often from another language (e.g. ⟨c⟩ in *scene* or ⟨h⟩ in *ghoul*); they mark a place where once there was an element–element correspondence. Some, however (like ⟨c⟩ in *scent* or ⟨h⟩ in *ghost*) are fakes—pseudo-fossils, erroneously introduced by etymologising orthographers. But whatever their origin, they are all genuine sequences. To describe any part of these digraphs as redundant *in its own medium* would make no sense. Indeed, whether fossil or fake, the grapheme translated by zero may serve as a positive clue for the translation of other elements in its environment. Though both ⟨ck⟩ and ⟨k⟩ are translated /k/, each conditions a different vowel in, for instance, 'backing: baking', 'licking: liking', etc.; and the difference between the presence and the absence of the untranslated letter serves to distinguish homonyms such as 'sent, cent, scent', 'knot, not', 'knew, new', etc.

Generally, digraphs present greater difficulties for the writer than for the reader. With the exception of ⟨th⟩ and ⟨sh⟩,[1] they generally compete with other (isophonic) 'transcriptions'; and the rules for selecting *them* rather than their rivals are often highly specific. Compare, for instance, the reading of 'redundancy digraphs' with their writing. For the reader of initial ⟨pn⟩ or ⟨kn⟩ the general phonological structure of English decides for translation by a single element (i.e. for recognition of a 'digraph'); and a simple phonotactic rule: 'initial ⟨p⟩ or ⟨k⟩ is silent before ⟨n⟩'—selects the particular element. For the writer, on the other hand, there is nothing but the reference to

---

elements is to be regarded as redundant. A spelling reform which might wish to remove one of them would have to decide which. The greater simplicity of the rules for translating ⟨s⟩ and ⟨k⟩ will argue for retaining *them* and declaring ⟨c⟩ redundant. (But see below about the *graphemic* function of the untranslated.)

[1] ⟨th⟩ and ⟨sh⟩ are exceptional in that the corresponding /θ,ð/ and /ʃ/ (in conditions which can be stated easily) have no other transcriptions; while of course /f/ corresponds to ⟨ph⟩ and ⟨f⟩, /n/ to ⟨kn⟩, ⟨gn⟩, ⟨n⟩, not to say anything of the confusing many-many relations between diphthongs and digraphs.

a particular word ('pneumonia', 'knot', etc.), to direct him to
⟨pn⟩ or ⟨kn⟩ rather than ⟨n⟩. There is, as one would say in
non-technical parlance, 'no rule'. It is in such cases, i.e. where
a translation-rule (such as it is) refers to quite specific lexical
conditions, that we might speak of 'logographic' and 'logophonic' conventions in the English writing system.

4.3.4. *Logographic and Logophonic Conventions.*

Apart from technical notations, the reading or writing of English words is never governed entirely by logographic conventions. There are no orthographic parallels to the obligatory
logographs of arithmetic ('3, 4, 0, + ', etc.), though it is of
course always possible to use some optional logographic alternatives to the orthography, and even to sanction such by convention (as in writing '&' for 'and' or '£' for 'pound'). But in
normal English orthography, even the most irregularly spelt
word is spelt partly by more general rules of phono-graphic
correspondence. No English word needs to be read purely by
'look and say', like the arithmetic symbols.[1] However, the reading or writing of *part* of a word is frequently governed by a
logographic rule; i.e. the translation (into phonemes or graphemes) of that part is controlled by its being part of a *particular
word*.

It seems important to distinguish two ways in which logographic rules may supervene upon the operation of more general
ones—and so to distinguish two kinds of logographic convention:

(i) one kind which provides *subsidiary* clues for selecting
among two or more regular translations, and

(ii) one which provides 'rules' to *override* more regular correspondences.

The latter seem to be the more disruptive. Though they affect
some very common words, they seem to have an especially
strong claim on the attention of spelling reformers.

Subsidiary Clues.— Logographic clues of the first, *subsidiary*,
kind are used when a *reader* of English has to decide how to

---

[1] Cp. D. H. Stott, *Roads to Literacy*, pp. 67ff., where the educational
implications are discussed.

sound written words like 'bow, row, sow; tear, read, wearing',
etc.[1] Generally, the native speaker will find it easy enough to
choose among the alternative isographic *soundings* ('that sow',
'they sow', 'he read')—though, occasionally, clues will not be
sufficient for determining the appropriate correspondence ('they
read'). Those learning to *write*, on the other hand, may be less
secure in choosing among different and equally regular isophonic shapes; they find it more difficult to remember which is
which in this 'second language' of theirs, the language of
letters: 'vein', 'vain' or 'vane'; 'sail' or 'sale'; 'feet' or 'feat';
'sent', 'cent' or 'scent'; 'no' or 'know'; 'write', 'right', 'wright'
or 'rite'—and very many more.

The graphemic discrimination of homophones is often cited
as one of the great advantages of written English over spoken.
It is a dubious advantage. If we remember the cost of having to
carry in memory many hundreds of specific selections, and consider that the gain is something that spoken English can easily
do without, the balance may not be very encouraging.[2]

In describing a translation-rule as 'logographic', we have been
making use of a traditional term—extending it to refer to *any*
translation correspondence which is tied to a *particular* lexical
unit. Strictly speaking, the term 'logographic' is appropriate
only to morpho-graphemic rules for reading. The analogous
morphophonemic conditions on which we rely for writing would
be properly described as 'logophonic'. Terminological precision
may here prevent some confusion. It would guard against
assuming that a logographic rule (for reading) must be paralleled
by a logophonic one (for spelling), or vice versa. There is, in
fact, no reason to expect such simple symmetry between the
two operations.

To be able to read ⟨bow⟩, we require a subsidiary logographic
rule to decide between /bəʊ/ and /baʊ/, while in the other
direction, /baʊ/ needs no logophonic rule to be written ⟨bow⟩;
the only 'regular' rival for ⟨ow⟩ to match /aʊ/ would be ⟨ou⟩,
which however is excluded from the final position. On the other

---

[1] The rule, on the other hand, which chooses between /'impɔt/ and
/im'pɔt/, /'kɒnvɪkt/ and /kən'vɪkt/, etc., is a more general rule, hence
not logographic.

[2] This throws doubt on some of Dr. Wijk's incidental proposals for
deliberate extensions of this game (*Regularized English*, pp. 69, 163, 180
and passim).

hand, the writer choosing between ⟨sale⟩ and ⟨sail⟩, or ⟨sent⟩ and ⟨cent⟩ etc. has to rely on logophonic clues; while, as in most cases of partially logographic writing, the reader's choices are here governed by general rule.

A very prominent example of such asymmetry is found in those many words which by various endings are marked as nouns or adjectives:

suspicion, musician, suspicious, luscious, efficient, ancient, special, conscience, patience, nation, pension, mansion, mission, passion, censure, pressure, invasion, decision, explosion, pleasure, etc., etc.

In order to read these, a fairly general morphographemic rule will be sufficient in almost every case. It will refer to the final sequences ⟨-ion, -ian, -ience, -ure; -ious, -ial, -ient⟩ as *graphemic markers* of nouns or adjectives which, as such, determine the reading of antecedent ⟨c, sc, ss, t⟩ to be /ʃ/, and the reading of ⟨s⟩ to be either /ʒ/ or /ʃ/ (according to whether it is preceded by a vowel-letter or not).[1] Translation into writing, on the other hand, requires supplementary logophonic clues. Having recognised the phonemic markers of nouns /-ʃn, -ʃn̩s, -ʃə; -ʒn̩, -ʒə/, or of adjectives /-ʃl̩, -ʃəs, -ʃn̩t/, general rule allows us to deter-

---

[1] Dr. Wijk tries to provide lower-level rules for the reader and refers to the purely graphemic sequences: ⟨ci, sci, si, ti, ssi, ce⟩. However, in order to provide for their reading he has to assume some rather problematic phonological features of the whole words to be already known: his contextual clues being 'in unstressed syllables, before the murmur vowel [ə]'; moreover, he is then left with a larger number of exceptions, which in fact require logographic listing. Avoidance of grammatical information seems to cause much unnecessary and unrealistic complication. As regards writing, we shall see that no simple *low-level* rule could be even approximately adequate. It would appear, then, that once more a significant grammatical condition has been missed, probably on account of an effort to avoid grammatical information.

It is interesting to note that the abstract lexico-phonological representations of Chomsky and Halle (op. cit.) will also miss the appropriate generalisations, though for the opposite reason (cp. p. 68, n.1, above). What we are given, here, is a great deal of interesting information about such words as *musician, relaxation, invasion*, possibly also something highly dubious about *mission* (mit+ion?), *nation* (nat+ion?), but nothing helpful at all about the relevant regularities of scores of words such as *passion, pension, mention, mansion, ancient*, etc.

It is true that ⟨-ion⟩ cannot easily be regarded as a suffix of 'nation' or 'pension', or ⟨-ient⟩ as a suffix of 'ancient': but both are grammatically significant *markers*—what J. R. Firth called 'exponents of a grammatical category'.

mine ⟨-ion (or -ian[1]) -ience, -ure⟩ (with ⟨s⟩ corresponding to /ʒ/) for nouns, and ⟨-ial, -ious, -ient⟩ for adjectives. But the choice between ⟨c, s, ss, sc, t⟩ requires subsidiary logophonic rules. When we learn to write /ræʃn/ and /pæʃn/; or /menʃn/ and /penʃn/; or/lʌʃəs/ and /sjupə'stɪʃəs/; or /speʃl/ and /paʃl/—what requires a special effort to remember is surely just the individual *logophonic supplementation* of the general morphophonemic rule. We have to learn: '/ræʃn/ to be written with ⟨t⟩' but '/pæʃn/, with ⟨ss⟩'; '/menʃn/, with ⟨t⟩' but '/penʃn/ with ⟨s⟩'; '/lʌʃəs/, with ⟨sc⟩', etc. We are not very likely to go wrong with the rest.[2]

We find, then, that while general morphographemic rules determine how these words are to be read aloud, no general morphophonemic rules can suffice for writing them down. But let us note that general morphological conditions control the translations in either direction. What we pick out to read is not plain ⟨c⟩ or ⟨s⟩ or ⟨t⟩ of, say, *suspicion, suspicious, pension, nation* nor even ⟨ci⟩, ⟨si⟩, ⟨ti⟩, etc., but always ⟨c, s, t⟩ *as determined by the following graphemic marker* of nouns or adjectives. This is why we are quick to learn that the first ⟨ti⟩ of *partition* or *superstitious* is not to be read like the second. Similarly, in learning to write, we do not learn to match /ʃ/ with ⟨c, s, t⟩, etc., except *where it is part of a morphophonemic marker*. This is why we are quick to grasp that the /ʃ/ of /lʌʃ/ 'lush' is not to

---

[1] The decision between ⟨-ion⟩ (*action, suspicion*) and ⟨-ian⟩ (*musician, Venetian*) is between the abstract 'it'-nouns and 'he/she'-nouns.

[2] It should also be noted that the regular graphemic markers (for reading) do not exactly correspond to the regular phonemic markers (for writing): the graphemic markers are preceded by a variable consonant-letter, while the phonemic markers include the regular /ʃ/ or /ʒ/. This also makes clear that in considering the *regular* polygraphy of /ʃ/ (as in *ship* or *machine*) we must ignore all those five graphic correspondents which are chosen by reference to irregular logophonic clues:

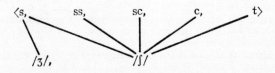

This is a difficulty for the writer. To the reader, the isophony of the five units presents little difficulty, and the single polyphony of /s/ is, as we have seen, resolved by a simple graphotactic rule.

be written like the /ʃ/ of /lʌʃəs/ 'luscious'. Only where /ʃ/ is part of a morphophonemic marker did we learn to match it with ⟨sc⟩. Indeed, in this case, we have learned to exclude ⟨sh⟩ from the permissible alternatives.

It again seems reasonable to suppose that educational tests would, on the whole, confirm the assumption that the more general rules are mastered with far greater ease than the specific ones. Such tests would also make it quite clear that those lists of phonographic correspondences which enumerate no less than twelve alternative graphic translations of /ʃ/ give us a highly distorted picture of English orthography.[1] No reader or writer of English should be supposed to be operating with the unsorted correspondences of those lists. There are lexicographical parallels to this aberration of orthographic listing in some obviously unhelpful dictionary entries. For example, it is quite common for a preposition in one language to be given from half a dozen to a dozen and more translations into another, and no indication of the syntactic rules which, in any particular case, restrict the choice.

Overriding Clues.— It is among logographic (and logophonic) rules of the other, *overriding*, kind that we encounter the true 'exceptions' of the orthography. We were getting rather near to such exceptions when, in examining the case of grammatical markers, we found a wide range of alternative translations (of /ʃ/ or /ʒ/) confined to certain morphological functions. However, that range, being conditioned by a general rule which refers to certain nouns and adjectives, is still seen to operate in a very large number of items. Utterly exceptional, on the other hand, are cases where a 'rule' determines a specific choice which *runs counter* to some more general rule. It is such an overriding logographic rule that mentions for instance 'bestial, bastion' as being read with /tj/ but 'Christian, question' as demanding either /tj/ or /tʃ/. And it is an overriding logophonic rule that asks for /kʊʃn/ to be written with ⟨sh⟩ (unless we may take this as a mark of its being a 'concrete noun' in /-ʃn/). Such 'rules' (conventions), which do not instruct us how to choose among more or less regular alternatives but override all of them, represent one of the most serious difficulties of English

---

[1] R. A. Hall lists (pp. 34f.): ⟨sh, ce, ch, ci, s, sch, sci, se, ss, ssi, ti⟩.

orthography. Numerous instances are found among the most common words:

do, does, are, could, should, you, who, one, two, any, many, women, come, blood, death, head, sure, sugar, friend, bury, busy, build, shoe, great, etc.

The list looks formidable. But we must not forget that in every case, the anomalous logographic clue is required only for translating *part* of the graphemic sequence, generally only one single phoneme. For a teacher to ignore this and plump for a pure 'look and say' (i.e. a purely logographic) approach to reading and writing, even of those words, is to throw away the majority of the clues. The correspondences ⟨w-men⟩ ↔ /w-mən/, ⟨fr-nd⟩ ↔ /fr-nd/, ⟨bl-d⟩ ↔ /bl-d/, ⟨d-th⟩ ↔ /d-θ/, etc., are all quite regular. They only need to be supplemented—though in a way which ignores the more regular correspondences between the two media. According to general rule, we should have to read ⟨friend⟩ to rhyme it with ⟨fiend⟩, ⟨blood⟩ to rhyme with ⟨mood⟩, and ⟨death⟩ with ⟨wreath⟩. The required phoneme (or grapheme) has to be chosen as just a marker of the individual word. It is like translating 'I bought strawberries' into German, or 'Ich habe Erdbeeren gekauft' into English, when we have to ignore the normal correspondences of 'straw' and 'Erde'.

It would be ludicrous (though such things do happen) for a German–English dictionary to list 'straw' among 'earth, ground, soil' as one of the various English translations of 'Erde', or vice versa to list 'Erde' as a German translation of 'straw'; while of course any dictionary would have to list the more regular correspondence of 'berry' with 'Beere'. It is equally inappropriate to list ⟨ie⟩ ↔ /e/, ⟨oo⟩ ↔ /ʌ/, ⟨u⟩ ↔ /i/, etc., as ordinary phonographic correspondences; but this is still general practice. As in the English–German translation, a specific rule must say that 'straw- *of strawberry*' is translated 'Erd-', so in phonographic translation, a specific (logographic) rule says that ⟨-ie-⟩ *of* ⟨friend⟩ is translated /e/ and ⟨-oo-⟩ *of* ⟨blood⟩ is translated /ʌ/. A match which is uniquely determined by some particular context must not be presented as independent from its context.

In most of these cases, the incidence of an overriding logographic clue is signalled by the *inapplicability* of any more

regular correspondence; in Standard English, the pronunciations */blud/ or */frind/ and the spellings *⟨blud⟩ and *⟨frend⟩
are as vacuous as are in English *earthberries, or in German
*Strohbeeren. This elimination of the regular translation is
obviously important for learning to read and write. The child
will frequently attempt a regular translation first, and only fall
back upon a specific 'look and say', when the first regular 'saying' has failed to make sense. Similarly, in writing, we are all
familiar with the expedient of putting down a tentative transcription merely to find out that it does not look like any
English word.

It is in such cases, then—when we have to rely on logographic
clues of one kind or the other—that, in learning to read, we
must fall back, in some degree, on 'look and say', and not
merely in the very general sense in which reading is *always*
'look and say'. It is of course true that our reading of a text, as
much as our listening to speech, is always powerfully assisted by
a global recognition of whole words and even whole phrases.
We do not really pick out every successive sound or letter; external circumstances (of noise, speed, clarity of writing, etc.) as
well as the reader's or listener's individual disposition determine in every instance how many analytic clues are given, and
how many of these are needed for the whole message to be
received. However, in the case of logographic clues, the orthography itself demands recognition of *specific* higher-level units
—demands it as a condition of phono-graphic translation. Here,
some measure of 'look and say' is not just optional or helpful
but obligatory.

As to the *extent* of such obligatory 'look and say' we have seen
that, for recognition of any word, English orthography offers at
least partial analytic clues. Exactly how much is given as regular, and how much needs to be supplied from our memory of
specific words, is however not always quite clear. The decision
will then be a practical matter. We shall notice those analytic
clues which are given by simple and fairly general rules, but
may ignore others. Thus, we shall certainly note the consonant-
letters in

⟨have, give, live, move, love, come, some, etc.⟩

But we should gain little by further confining the logographic translation in the case of ⟨have⟩ or ⟨give⟩ or ⟨live⟩ to choosing between two regular readings—namely:

(i) ⟨a-e⟩ →/eɪ/ as in ⟨save, crave⟩, or
    ⟨i-e⟩ →/aɪ/ as in ⟨strive, five⟩, and
(ii) ⟨ve⟩ →/v/ as in ⟨leave, mauve⟩.

For, the same treatment would fail with the analogous ⟨move, love, come, some⟩. It will be simpler, then, in all these cases, to choose the vowel by an overriding logographic rule; and we may assume that a reader is doing this.

Similarly, there is nothing to be gained by trying to restrict the logographic translation of the notorious English sequence ⟨ough⟩: to (redundant) ⟨gh⟩ in *bough, plough*; to ⟨u⟩ (redundant) in *cough, trough*; to ⟨ou⟩ →/ʌ/ in *enough, rough, tough*, etc. Instead of applying the logographic decision to a different part in every case, we shall better apply it always to the same whole sequence ⟨ough⟩, the regular phonographic translation being confined to the consonantal onset of the words. But it will be worthwhile to remember all those 'strong' verbs with 'preterite' ⟨t⟩ as a group: *bought, brought, fought, thought*, etc.

This is, after all, how in ordinary translation we should deal with formulaic sequences—with phrases like 'take advantage of, take care, take comfort, take liberties, take pity on, take a seat, take effect', etc. In many of these, there are parts which could be matched by another language in accordance with some general tendency of correspondence; but it will not always be the same part, and translation of the rest will in every case presuppose recognition of the phrase as a whole.[1] It is less troublesome then, in every case, to translate the phrase as a whole.

4.3.5. *Applications*

A survey of the various controlling conditions of phonographic translation shows clearly that in order to be literate in English it is not enough to know about its sounds and letters. The clues

---

[1] German translations, for instance, would be (with any separately translatable English words given in brackets): sich zu*nutze* machen (advantage), sich in Acht *nehmen* (take), sich trösten (—), sich *Freiheiten* heraus*nehmen* (take liberties), *Mitleid* haben mit (pity), *Platz nehmen* (take-seat), in Kaft treten (—).

on which we have to rely are very largely of a higher level. An English text cannot be read aloud, and English speech cannot be written down, without some measure of comprehension. This demanding nature of English orthography is not always adequately appreciated. To become literate in terms of the traditional orthography *must* take longer than it would to acquire a more or less phonetic technique of writing (such as i.t.a.). But much of the time would be spent on learning something about the English language. This will be so especially if the regular spellings are taught in a way which reveals their grammatical and lexical conditions—that is, if they are *not* taught, all of them, as just some sort of faulty phonetic transcription.[1]

It is of course no argument *against* a phonetically more regular script, such as i.t.a., that it permits us to read without comprehension (to 'bark at print'). This is what an approximately phonemic orthography is bound to permit. Any revision of the English orthography will aim at reducing its dependence on grammatical and lexical clues. Correct translation on the phonological level would then, to a greater extent, *guarantee* an adequate match on higher levels, rather than depend on it. But if social conditions and cultural traditions prevent us from using an optimally efficient script, which in any case would not be phonemic, it will be well to remember that the special efforts which are imposed on us by the traditional English orthography need not by any means all be wasted.

The learner will have to concentrate on those very large sections which are rule-governed, rational, and fairly easy to master. It is in the frequent need of subsidiary logographic clues, and—what is even worse—in the intrusion of *overriding* logographic conventions, that we find the greatest defects of

---

[1] It is precisely this informative part of the non-phonetic English orthography that Dr. Wijk wishes to preserve. We should expect, of course, that the reading of *isolated* words will be much more difficult in the traditional morphographemic orthography than it is in a *phonetically* more regular script. The contextual clues on which the former relies are represented only very imperfectly within the compass of a single word. This may well explain why children trained through i.t.a. would, after their transfer to the traditional orthography, perform better on a Word Spelling Test, while those trained exclusively in the traditional way would often be more proficient in a Reading Comprehension Test. (Cp. J. Downing, *Evaluating the Initial Teaching Alphabet.*) The current reading and writing tests seem to be generally biased in favour of context-free recognition.

F*

English orthography. The alphabetic principle is all but given up, when it becomes necessary for us to know and recognise a *specific word* before we can read or write it. These defects are not so numerous as they are prominent. And as it is wrong when training someone in the grammatical habits of a language to ignore the rules and to concentrate on the exceptions; so in teaching children or foreigners to read or write English, it would be wrong to forget, while drawing attention to what is specific and irregular, that sensitivity to the regularities, too, needs to be awakened. In this respect, much of our teaching is bound to be imperfect at present—simply because the regularities of English orthography have not been stated adequately. Writers of school-primers and teachers are in need of such a statement—not of course in order to teach it, but in order to derive from it a clearer awareness of those skills of translation which they are called upon to develop.

A similar detailed study of orthographic structure is required for projects of *mechanical* transcription and transdiction. We have the computers and we have the machines for synthetic speech; but we do not know how to programme them for efficient phonographic translation.

Finally, there are the various projects for reforming the established orthography itself. No such project can be taken seriously so long as it is not based on a detailed analysis of the established conventions. The prevailing orthographic rules need to be viewed as involving the structure of the language as a whole; and they need to be graded, not only according to incidence and overall frequency but also according to their relative simplicity and generality. This alone can provide us with the linguistic evidence which, in conjunction with social and cultural considerations, would determine the appropriate limits of orthographic reform.

4.4. THE UNTRANSLATABLE

The relation between writing and speech is ordinary translatability also in this respect: that information given in either medium is not always translatable into the other.

No medium or language is entirely neutral. What is expressed in one may be incapable of being expressed in another. Disparity in the very receptiveness of different media must be distinguished from casual non-conformity. Any merely incidental lack of correspondence between the elements of two media can be cured by extending the stock of expressions in one medium or the other; the inventory of expressions is subject to historical change. An element which is current in one medium and only incidentally without correspondent in another can be matched with a novel sequence, an unusual loan-translation or a metaphor. But nothing can be done about the kind of essential discorrespondence which is due simply to the difference between two media. There is no cure for those comparative deficiencies of speech and writing, which are due to the fact that speech takes time while writing occupies space.

On the one hand—the temporal sequence of sounds, all merging into one another, and each recognisable for but a split-second before it disappears irrecoverably: their musical organisation by stress- and tone-patterns and by changes of tempo cannot be matched adequately with any linear sequence of discrete letters. On the other hand—strings of abiding letters, each of them fixed at regular intervals: their clear organisation by a periodic intervention of empty spaces of varying size and by the bracketings of exactly located punctuations can find nothing in speech adequately to match it. It is not surprising then that each of the two media has developed preferences for different types of message. Anybody who has had to 'read a paper' or to 'write a talk' (possibly to be broadcast as well as printed) knows how difficult it is to find a style which is tolerably well suited for both purposes. In these days of tape-recordings, the essential difference between writing and speech has become even more obvious. It is quite common for a perfectly intelligible recorded talk or conversation to be incapable of intelligible transcription. The inevitable absence of adequate graphic signals for patterns of stress or tone and for changes of tempo leaves much of the transcribed remainder obscure. What is required here for expression in writing is complete reformulation—'free' translation.

Once more the lexical parallels are striking. As the submorphemic signals of writing and speech are subject to the inevitable restrictive force of their respective physical media, so in ordinary translation the significant expressions of two languages are subject to the inevitable constraints of their respective phonologies and grammars. As phonemes and graphemes are embedded in different physical media, so the words of the source and those of the target-language are embedded in different phonological and grammatical structures. The translator, then, is bound to encounter instances of essential discorrespondence—problems which (except for some stroke of luck) must be every bit as insoluble as would be an attempt to translate a pun. Indeed, there are many spoken puns which are incapable of translation into writing. 'He insists upon his /raɪts/' could be a sharp pun in a controversy in which rights are claimed in defence of obnoxious rites. But how can one put it in English orthography?[1] Similarly, how is one to translate a pair of rhyming lines (and thoughts) from English into French, when rhyming is a rare distinction in English, but is frequent and cheap in French? How does one translate the alliteration and consonantal rhyme of 'last but not least' into any other language? Or, what other language could possibly match the expressiveness of Milton's eccentric syntax, when its very eccentricity can appear only against the background of the normal *English* syntax?

Translators are familiar with a host of such problems. Frequently, their 'free translation' consists in simply accepting a loss in one place, and trying to compensate for it in another. Having missed some quality of the source, they try to make up by some distinctive and perhaps equally untranslatable quality of the target-language—in much the same way as the empty spaces and punctuations of writing do not correspond to, but make up for the loss of the prosodic features of speech.

There are also intermediate styles of speaking and reading— uses of a language, as it were, which rely on bilingualism. There is a peculiar reading-style of written English, which tries, as far as possible, to superimpose a separate convention of discrete words and of punctuating intonations upon the organisation of normal spoken English. This mixed language is meant to miti-

---

[1] An interesting remedy may be found at times in relying on 'bilingualism'. When one meaning is less normal than the other, this will be the one given in writing, the assumption being that in reading aloud the more normal meaning will suggest itself—e.g. in the following cartoon-caption from a daily (picturing a happy couple, the man speaking): 'We are happy courting. Why altar it?'

gate at least some of the defects of speech vis-à-vis writing. Equally common are special graphic conventions which aim at counteracting the comparative imperfections of normal writing. Poets, having to write in toneless letters which cannot show rhyme or tune or rhythm or tempo, must, in order that the poem's qualities may appear, rely on our reading it aloud. Having given us an imperfect translation of speech they ask us to re-translate it into the original. Some attempt will be made to supply certain deficiencies of writing; a number of additional visual conventions (line-ends, stanzas, dots, unusual empty spaces, etc.) are superimposed upon the normal organisation of prose writing. At the same time, the poet may make use of some distinctive advantages of the medium of writing. Modern verse is very largely 'bilingual'.

'Media' are much discussed at present. As the spoken word has come to rival and surpass the written in what had long been the latter's special privilege—*publicity*, the increasing concurrence of the two media has made us only more intensely aware of the difference between them. That this difference is far from being trivial is not what one had expected; and the shock of the discovery is currently producing a great deal of mystification about 'media'. And yet, it is not surprising that messages which are linked by translation should fail to be equivalent. Approximation is all one may expect, even if the translation operates with units apparently so insignificant as sounds and letters.

BIBLIOGRAPHY

Aristotle—On Interpretation

—Poetics

Bazell, C. E.—'The Grapheme', in Hamp, E. P. (ed.), *Readings in Linguistics*, Vol. II, University of Chicago Press, 1966

Berko, Jean—'The Child's Learning of English Morphology', in Saporta, S. (ed.), *Psycho-linguistics, a Book of Readings*, New York, 1961

Bolinger, D. L.—'Visual Morphemes', *Language*, 1946

Brice, W. C.—'The Decipherment of the Minoan Script B and the Problem of the Linear Script A', in *Man*, 1957

Bywater, I.—*Aristotle, on the Art of Poetry* (translation and commentary), Oxford, 1909

Catford, J. C.—*A Linguistic Theory of Translation*, Oxford University Press, 1965

Chao, Y. R.—'Graphic and Phonetic Aspects of Linguistic and Mathematical Symbols', in *Structure of Language and its Mathematical Aspects*, Proceedings and Symposia in Applied Mathematics, Vol. XII, American Mathematical Society, Providence, 1961

Chomsky, N. and Halle, M.—*The Sound Pattern of English*, New York, 1968

Chou En Lai—*Reform of the Chinese Written Language*, Foreign Languages Press, Peking, 1958

Diogenes Laertius—*Lives and Opinions of the Philosophers*, Bk. VII, *Zeno*

Dixon, R. M. W.—*Linguistic Science and Logic*, The Hague, 1963

Donatus—*Ars Grammatica*

Downing, J.—*Evaluating the Initial Teaching Alphabet*, Cassell, London, 1967

Edfeldt, A. W.—*Silent Speech and Silent Reading*, Acta Universitatis Stockholmiensis, 1959

Firth, J. R.—*Papers in Linguistics*, Longmans, 1957

Follick, M.—*The Case for Spelling Reform*, Pitman and Sons, London, 1965

Gleason, H. A. Jr.—*Linguistics and English Grammar*, Holt, Reinhart and Winston Inc., 1963

Grumach, E.—'Der Ägäische Schriftkreis', in *Studium Generale*, Vol. 12 (1965)

Haas, W.—'On Spelling and Spelling Reform', in *Alphabets for English*, Mont Follick Series, Vol. 1, Manchester University Press, 1970

—'Grammatical Prerequisites of Phonological Analysis', in Hamm, J. (ed.), *Phonologie der Gegenwart*, H. Böhlaus Nachf., 1967

—'The Theory of Translation', in G. H. R. Parkinson (ed.), *The Theory of Meaning*, Oxford University Press, 1968

Hall, R. A. Jr.—*Sound and Spelling in English*, Chilton Books, 1961, 1966

—*Introductory Linguistics*, Chilton Books, 1964

Halle, M. and Chomsky, N.—*The Sound Pattern of English*, New York, 1968

Harrison, M.—*Instant Reading*, Pitman and Sons, London, 1964

Hjelmslev, L.—*Prolegomena to a Theory of Language*, University of Wisconsin Press, Madison, 1963

Hockett, C. F.—*A Manual of Phonology*, Indiana University Publications, Baltimore, 1955

Jakobson, R.—*Selected Writings*, vol. 1, Mouton, 1962

MacCarthy, P. A. D.—'New Spelling with Old Letters', in *Alphabets for English*, Mont Follick Series, Vol. 1, Manchester University Press, 1970

Martinet, A.—'Un ou deux Phonèmes?' in Hamp, E. P. (ed.), *Readings in Linguistics*, Vol. II., University of Chicago Press, 1966

—*Éléments de Linguistique Générale*, Armand Collin, 1960; English version, Faber and Faber, London, 1964

McIntosh, A.—'The Analysis of Middle English', *Transactions of the Philological Society*, 1965

—'Graphology and Meaning', ' A Four-Letter word in Lady Chatterley's Lover', in *Patterns of Language*, Longmans, 1966

Moulton, W. G.—'The Short Vowel Systems of Northern Switzerland', *Word*, 16.2, 1960

Mountford, J.—*i. t. a. as a Grading Device*, Reading Research Document No. 5, University of London Institute of Education

Pitman, I. J.—'The Assault on the Conventional Alphabets and Spelling', in *Alphabets for English*, Mont Follick Series, Vol. i, Manchester University Press, 1970
—'Learning to Read', *Journal of the Royal Society of Arts*, 1961
Postal, P. M.—Review of Dixon, 'Linguistic Science and Logic', *Language*, 1966
Priscianus—*Institutiones Grammaticae*
de Saussure, F.—*Cours de Linguistique Générale*, Paris, 1922; English translation, Philosophical Library, New York, 1959
Smalley, W. A. and others—*Orthography Studies*, United Bible Societies, 1964
Spache, G.—'Critical Analysis of Various Methods of Classifying Spelling Errors', *The Journal of Educational Psychology*, Vol. 31 (1960)
Stott, D. H.—*Roads to Literacy*, Glasgow, 1965
Vachek, J.—'Zum Problem der geschriebenen Sprache' (1939) in *A Prague School Reader in Linguistics*, Indiana University Press, 1964
—'Some Remarks on Writing and Phonetic Transcription', in Hamp, E. P. (ed.), *Readings in Linguistics*, Vol. II, University of Chicago Press, 1966
Weissgerber, L.—*Die Verantwortung für die Schrift*, Dudenverlag, 1964
Wijk, A.—*Rules of Pronunciation for the English Language*, Oxford University Press, 1966
—*Regularized English*, Acta Universitatis Stockholmiensis VII, Almqvist and Wiksell, Stockholm, 1959
—'Regularized English, The only practicable solution of the English Spelling Reform Problem', in *Alphabets for English*, Manchester University Press, 1970

INDEX

Allerton, D. J., 6
Allographs, *see* Graphemes
Allophones, *see* Phonemes
Alphabet, *see* Writing; *also*
    Phonetic transcription; Ortho-
    graphic conventions; Spelling
    reform; 'Teaching Alphabets'
Ambiguity and equivalence, 20f,
    47f, 72, 76f
Aristotle, 10f, 13, 27

Bazell, C. E., 6, 15, 48
Berko, Jean, 5
Bilingualism, *see* Translation
Bolinger, D. L., 13
Brice, W. C., 28
Bywater, I., 27f

Catford, J. C., 19
Chandley, J., 65
Chao, Y. R., 37f
Chinese orthography, 29, 33f, 37f
Chomsky, N., 20, 68, 77f
Chou En Lai, 33f
Computer, reading by, 2, 34, 84;
    translating by, 30, 59
Cruttenden, A., 6

Decipherment, 28
Dialects, 18f, 39
Digraphs and diphones, 42, 44ff,
    71f
Diogenes Laertius, 24, 27
Dixon, R. M. W., 12
Donatus, 24
Downing, J., 53, 56, 83

Edfeldt, A. W., 12
English orthography: and English
    Dialects, 39; and the English
    speaking child, 20, 37; and the
    foreigner, 5, 38f, 65f; digraphs,
    71ff; 'logographic' features of,
    29, 75ff; *see also* Orthographic
    conventions; Phonographic cor-
    respondence; Grammar and
    orthography; Spelling reform;
    Reading and writing

Equivalence (of graphemes), *see*
    Ambiguity and equivalence

Firth, J. R., 28, 76
Follick, M., 38f
French, M. A., 6
French orthography, 52f
Frequency of phonographic corre-
    spondences, 60ff

German orthography, 35
Gleason, H. A., 35
Grammar and orthography, 3f,
    58ff, 64ff, 68ff, 76ff
Graphemes, 7f, 24ff; and digraphs,
    44ff; isophonic ('equivalent')
    and polyphonic ('ambiguous'),
    9, 20ff, 50ff, 56ff; recognition
    and realisation of, 31f, 33ff, 72;
    see also Letter; Phonographic
    correspondence; Phonographic
    divergence
Graphotactic Rule, 59; *see* Rules
    of phonographic translation—
    contextual
Grumach, E., 28

Hall, R. A., Jr., 10, 12, 16, 57, 60, 79
Halle, M., 12, 20, 68ff, 77
Handwriting, 34, 36
Harrison, M., 39
Hjelmslev, L., 12f
Hockett, C. F., 48
Homonymity, *see* Ambiguity and
    equivalence
Homophony and homography, *see*
    Ambiguity and equivalence

Ideograms, *see* Writing; Logo-
    graphic and logophonic conven-
    tions
Idioms, 46ff
Isographic, *see* Phonemes
Isophonic, *see* Graphemes
i.t.a., 33, 53ff, 62, 69, 83; *see also*
    Pitman, Sir James

Jakobson, R., 12f

James, K., 6, 65

Letter—shape (*figura*) and name (*nomen*), 14f, 24ff, 34f; value (*potestas*), 27f; 'silent', 37, 45, 63, 74f, 82; *see also* Graphemes; Digraphs and diphones; Segmentation
Lexical incidence, *see* Frequency of phonographic correspondences
Linear A and Linear B, 28
Logographic and logophonic conventions, 29, 57, 75ff; *see also* English orthography; Grammar and orthography; Orthographic conventions; Writing
'Look and Say', 75, 80, 82

MacCarthy, P. A. D., 6, 33, 36, 62
Markers, *see* Grammar and orthography
Martinet, A., 48, 52
McIntosh, A., 9, 11, 14ff, 16, 47, 58
Meaning : and translation, 17f; of texts, written or spoken, 10ff; 'phonic', 14f
Morphographemic and morphophonemic rules, 59f, 76; *see also* Rules of phonographic translation, logographic and logophonic
Moulton, W. G., 61
Mountford, J., 55
Music, 13

'New Spelling', 62

Orthographic conventions: biased for reading, 52ff, 65; irregular, 43f, 75ff; regular, 43, 60ff; Standard of correctness, 19, 32, 50, 59; *see also* English orthography; Grammar and orthography; Phonographic correspondence; Phonographic divergence; Spelling reform; Rules of phonographic translation; Writing

Phonemes, 7f, 24ff; polygraphic and isographic, 21f, 53ff, 56f; recognition and realisation of, 31f, 36ff; *see also* Sound; Phonographic correspondence; Phonographic divergence

Phonetic (Phonemic) transcription, 3ff, 7, 14, 25, 43; *see also* Orthographic conventions; Writing
'Phonic Method', 49
Phonographic correspondence, 7ff, 25ff; and discorrespondence, 85ff; as reference, 9ff, 24; as translatability, 16ff; disjunctive, 44ff; lists, 57, 79ff; *see also* English orthography; Phonographic divergence
Phonographic divergence, 4ff, 8f, 44ff, 52f, 56; and ambiguity, 9f, 20f, 47f, 71f, 76f; and divergent translations, 20f; kinds of, 44ff; weighting of, 6f, 68ff; *see also* Phonographic correspondence
Phonotactic Rule, 59; *see also* Rules of phonographic translation, contextual
Pitman, Sir James, 35, 38, 53ff, 68f; *see also* i.t.a.
Plato, 27
Poetry, spoken and written, 13f, 36, 41, 85ff
Polygraphic, *see* Phonemes
Polyphonic, *see* Graphemes
Postal, P. M., 12
Priscian, 24, 28
Prosodic features and punctuation, 36, 65, 85ff
Punctuation, *see* Prosodic features and punctuation

Reading and writing—automatic, 2, 34, 84; silent, 12, 30; teaching of, 4f, 30f, 37ff, 60, 63f, 66f, 68f, 71, 83f; the operations, 3, 17f, 31ff, 42ff, 68f, 71; unequal difficulties, 4f, 42, 50ff, 56, 65, 74f, 76ff; *see also* Computer; English orthography; Teaching alphabets; Translation
Reference, of grapheme to phoneme, *see* Phonographic correspondence
Regularity, orthographic, *see* Orthographic conventions; Rules of phonographic translation; Frequency of phonographic correspondence
'Regularized English', 56, 60ff, 64f, 68f, 76f; *see also* Spelling Reform; Wijk, A.

Representation of phonemes, *see* Phonographic correspondence

Rules of phonographic translation: and tendencies, 6off; contextual, 63ff; lographic and logophonic, 75ff; same-level and higher-level, 58, 68f; simplicity and generality of, 63f, 68f, 77f; transformational, 20, 67ff; *see also* Translation, rules

Russian orthography, 44, 46

De Saussure, F., 13

Segmentation, 46; *see also* Handwriting; Sequence and pseudo-sequence

Sequence and pseudo-sequence, 45ff, 71ff, 82

Shaw, G. B., 35f, 57

Sign, arbitrariness of the, 13

'Simpler Spelling Association', 62

'Simplified Spelling Society', 61f

Smalley, W. A., 4

Sound—*figura*, 24; *nomen*, 15, 24f; *potestas*, 27f, 41; *see also* Phonemes

Spache, G., 5, 67

Spelling mistakes, 5f, 67; *see* Tests, educational

Spelling Reform—the aims, 2, 38f, 52ff, 83f; the task, 55, 61f, 64f, 67ff, 68f, 74, 79, 84; new letters, 33, 35f; *see* Reading and writing; Orthographic conventions; 'i.t.a.', 'New Spelling', 'Regularized English'

Standard, *see* Orthographic conventions; Dialects

Stott, D. H., 39, 75

Stress, 65; *see also* Prosodic features and punctuation

Style—spoken *versus* written, 85ff; *see also* Writing and speech

Suprasegmental features, *see* Prosodic features and punctuation

Synonymity, *see* Ambiguity and equivalence

'Teaching alphabets', 53ff; *see also* i.t.a.; Reading and writing

Tests, educational, 5f, 65, 67ff, 69, 79, 83; *see* Spelling mistakes

Transformations, *see* Rules of phonographic translation

Translation, 17ff, 40ff; automatic, 30, 59; and dictionaries, 50, 56f, 79f; clues, 56ff, 69f; difficulties, 42, 60, 68f; direction of, 42, 50ff; element/element and element/sequence, 46ff; free, 86; interlingual and intermedial, 17ff, 30ff, 43f, 46ff, 50, 59, 72; levels of, 18f; limits of, 85ff; loan translation, 73; of idioms and formulae, 46ff, 80f, 82; rules, 58f, 62f, 69f; *see also* Rules of phonographic translation

Untranslatable, 85ff; *see* Writing and speech

Vachek, J., 3, 11, 14, 32, 37

Weissgerber, L., 35

Wijk, A., 38, 57, 60ff, 83; *see also* Regularized English

Writing, 9ff; alphabetic, 3ff, 37f, 58; non-alphabetic, 28f, 33f, 75; ancient theories of, 10f, 24, 27f; *see also* Orthographic conventions; Phonetic transcription; Reading and writing; Writing and speech

Writing and speech, 36f; a kind of bilingualism, 2, 22, 42f, 87; priority of speech, 11f; untranslatability between, 13, 36, 43, 85ff; *see also* Phonographic correspondence; Translation; Writing